DALE B. J. RANDALL

"Theatres of Greatness": A Revisionary View of Ford's
Perkin Warbeck

EIS
EDITIONS

ELS Editions
Department of English
University of Victoria
Victoria, BC
Canada V8W 3W1
www.elseditions.com

Founding Editor: Samuel L. Macey

General Editor: Luke Carson

Printed by CreateSpace

English literary studies monograph series
ISSN 0829-7681 ; 37
ISBN-10 0-920604-27-7
ISBN-13 978-0-920604-27-4

To
Myron William Randall, Sr.
and
Frances Ann Delaplaine Randall

Fructum habet caritas.

CONTENTS

ILLUSTRATIONS

I am Richard II. know ye not that?

Elizabeth to William Lambarde (1601), cited in John Nichols, *The Progresses and Public Processions of Queen Elizabeth*, III (1823), 552.

Thus Text and Time due sute, and whilst you tell
Your Tale, wee'l easily find a Parallell.

John Quarles, "Upon the Incomparable Tragedy Called *Mirza*," in Robert Baron, *Mirza* (1647), A3v.

If intercourse in civill commerce may conduce to form the Judgement, compose the mind, or rectify the manners (as none who hath receiv'd impression there of, can deny) no form of institution humane reason can reflect upon, more suddenly and more perfectly can attain thereto, than can the well composed illustrations of a *Theater*.

Leonard Willan, "The Epistle Dedicatory," *Orgula* (1658), A4v.

PROLOGUE

For a work which is generally and rightly placed among the finest of all English history plays, Ford's *Perkin Warbeck* has somehow drifted surprisingly free of its historical moorings. Since our views of it as conveyed in critical commentary often seem peculiarly blurred, and since it is a truism no longer in need of much arguing that a history play reflects both the age it depicts and its own age, it follows that the drift of *Perkin Warbeck* may have hindered our seeing it clearly. The understanding with which each age and each person within that age will "see" this play or any other varies infinitely, of course, because our knowledge is forever relative to what we already know. Nevertheless, since one of the things that many of us think we know is that plays reflect their own times, no matter what else they depict, we had better do our best to understand their reflections. The problem of proper dating opens up fundamental questions of subject and theme.

Having reviewed the facts in the case of *Perkin Warbeck*, G. E. Bentley has concluded that "Evidence for dating the play is negligible."[1] Given some latitude regarding what may be admissible as evidence, however, the present essay will try to show that we are not so bereft as this might suggest. The major external facts we have are the licensing and publication of the play in 1634. Hence Mildred Struble, writing in 1926, was moved to recall King Charles's failed foreign policy and to argue that Ford as a member of the Middle Temple was voicing the view of the legal profession against Stuart absolutism and divine right.[2] Thirty years later, Clifford Leech and Irving Ribner still found Ford's stance in the play to be Caroline.[3] Agreeing with Struble, Ribner wrote: "we must note that there is some subtle questioning of the doctrine of the divine right of kings which Charles I was so flagrantly abusing at the time the play was being written..." (p. 300). This is not the place to list those who have assumed that the play was published rather soon after its composition, but for good measure one might cite Philip Edwards ("Charles was betraying the monarchy"); Matthew Wikander (the character of "Perkin offers the romance ideal of the king as lover, an idea reflective of the attitude prevalent in the court of Charles I"); and Dorothy Farr ("The play is typically Caroline").[4]

On the other hand, Peter Ure, who likewise places the play in the 1630s, also observes that "There is, of course, nothing impossible in the supposition that the play was written quite soon after the publication of

11

its second major source ... in 1622."[5] That is, the search for hard evidence gives us not only 1634 as *terminus ad quem* but also, as *terminus a quo*, 1622—the year of Bacon's *Historie of the Raigne of King Henry the Seventh*. Like Ure, Donald Anderson also seems intrigued by the possibility of tracing the play to the 1620s, though he, too, decides on a date closer to 1634.[6]

Besides the date 1634 on the title page of the play, there is also the tantalizing notation "Acted (some-times) by the Queenes / MAIESTIES Servants at the / *Phoenix* in *Drurie* lane." Unfortunately, this assures us neither when nor by whom the play was first performed. It does tell us that *Perkin Warbeck* was produced by Queen Henrietta's Men at the Cockpit, or Phoenix, adjoining Drury Lane, some time between 1625 and 1634. It does not claim, however, that the play was introduced at that place or in that time-span. Moreover, even within that time-span the word "some-times," as was pointed out at least as early as 1811,[7] is a slippery token. Perhaps in the present context it is most likely to mean "formerly." As a matter of fact, since it is used within the play itself to refer to an earlier period, a possible question there might be *how much* earlier? Frion is described as "sometimes secretary" to Henry VII, "But Perkin's tutor now" (I.iii.49-51). If for the sake of argument we attempt to be historically accurate, then it would appear that Frion entered Henry's service in 1485 and left it about 1489, some half-dozen years before Warbeck and his crew arrived on the Kentish coast.

In any case, making use of this word "some-times" as part of his evidence, Alfred Harbage (who was seconded a few years later by Sidney Homan) suggested that Ford collaborated with Dekker on the play sometime in the 1620s.[8] Among other matters, Harbage was struck by the use of the name "Warbeck" in *The Witch of Edmonton* (1621), a drama on which Ford is known to have collaborated with Dekker and Rowley. There the name is given to a sort of country roaring boy who swears "By the honour of gentility" (I.ii.51). Subsequently, however, and rather persuasively, Ure refuted any claim of such collaboration on *Perkin Warbeck* by explaining the unlikelihood of Dekker's involvement in the play.[9] Nevertheless, on the positive side, one might observe that we have now accumulated here a small nucleus of scholars who are willing to entertain the idea that *Perkin Warbeck* was a product of the 1620s.

Assuming that history, when represented by any writer, both becomes and is shaped by that writer's present, let us proceed next to consider three details from *Perkin Warbeck* that cast shadows on the general assumption that the play is Caroline. First, the chief advisor to Warbeck,

Stephen Frion, a man whose duplicity serves as a foil to heighten Warbeck's better qualities, is described by the Bishop of Durham (a graybeard we can trust) as "French both in heart and actions!" (I.iii.53). The question at the moment is: what does "French" mean here? Probably it is not the sort of epithet that a conservative, politically sensitive royalist—as we shall see Ford to have been—would be expected to set down in such a context after 1624. And the epithet is reinforced moments later by King Henry himself. In the opening scene of the play Ford previously has had Henry decry "French dissimulation" (l. 112); and now Henry calls Frion a "subtle villain" and a "Pestilent adder" who "will hiss out poison / As dang'rous as infectious ..." (I.iii.51, 66-68). Even granting that Charles's queen was herself not always in sympathy with France, this is very strong talk. Pointing as it does to some puzzling and provocative issues, it may serve to alert us to still other striking facts about the play.

A second detail. When Dalyell is speaking of his ancestors, he has occasion to refer "To him that first begot the race of Jameses / That sway the sceptre to this very day" (I.ii.32-33). To this very day? More than likely a dual present is invoked here. One part is operative within the play (where Dalyell's listeners do not really need to be reminded who their monarch is), and one reaches out to remind the audience in the theater that their own monarch, who is a James, is part of that long line of Jameses represented onstage.[10]

A third clue is the striking praise that Henry VII has for the Spanish monarchs. Henry speaks of "wise Queen Isabel" and King Ferdinand, "who almost / Comes near a miracle in his success..." (II.iii.3, 9-10). Such words are explicable in their context if the time is 1490—or 1622 or 1623. It stands to reason, however, that after Charles had begun clamoring for war with Spain, and especially after February, 1624, when the English sent an ambassador to start negotiations for the marriage of Charles to the French Princess Henrietta Maria, Ford is less likely to have depicted an English king who even goes so far as to proclaim that "We, for our part, / Will imitate" the king of Spain (III.iii.12-13). Thanks to the efforts of George Villiers, the Duke of Buckingham, James's powerful favorite, hispaniolized counsellors were gradually thinned out in 1624-1625, and between 1625 and 1630 England was at war with Spain. Subsequently, it must be acknowledged, Charles tried to take a neutral course, eventually even moving toward a pro-Spanish position, but there is nothing in his reign—as there certainly is in James's—to parallel the Spanish-related events and enthusiasm in Ford's play.

13

CHAPTER ONE

A History Couched in a Play

With the passage of time, historical events, like works of art, acquire shifting horizons of meaning: Joan of Arc and the Charge of the Light Brigade have looked different in different periods. With regard to Ford's play, itself now a part of seventeenth-century literary history, and therefore subject to a wide variety of approaches, we have what this study will endeavor to show is a peculiarly 1620s image of a 1490s past. Since a literal depiction of past events is impossible in any form, obviously including historical drama, it follows that both the depicting work and the history depicted are going to be shaped in particular ways. It will always be impossible, of course, to discern all these ways, and for a variety of reasons, including the fact that any critic or literary historian who turns to Ford's historical materials will have his own misleading "idols." King James himself experienced the frustration of having his historical poem on the Battle of Lepanto miserably misunderstood even in his own time. The aim at this point, then, is to caution that even if we do engage in this sort of enterprise, we should understand that when all is said and done we will still only partially understand.

Misperceptions about *Perkin Warbeck* have long included the notion that it is not a history play. In 1935 M. Joan Sergeaunt wrote that "Ford is not really concerned at all with the fortunes of England, with its traditions, its politics and its countryside; of these he treats solely because of their effect on the somewhat fantastic character... that chance has called on to play... for a short while in the historical scene."[1] David Cecil agreed in 1957: "Ford... took little interest in the political implications of his theme."[2] And perhaps most amazingly of all, Winston Weathers in 1964: "the play... is no more concerned with 'kingship and government' that is the *Oedipus Tyrannus*."[3] All of this requires us to ignore the play's title, which proclaims the work a *Chronicle History*, and to gainsay the contemporary confirmation of Ford's friend Brograve, who complimented the dramatist on having written something called a "Chronicle History."[4] At the same time we remain critically alert to the frustrating, polonian amorphousness of Renaissance dramatic labels, and, indeed, to the generic mingling of elements in the works themselves, we should keep in mind also the opening words of Ford's Prologue: "Studies have of this nature been of late / ... out of fashion" (ll. 1-2). Whoever believes that this does not refer to histories for the stage ought to help us by saying what earlier genre is intended. Whoever believes so should also comment on what is meant when the Prologue goes on to observe that the "author" here "shows a history couched in a play..." (ll. 11-14). How can such a nay-saying reader account for the fact that on at least two occasions in the eighteenth century the play appears to have been revived in order to make political statements? Of course the aim here is not to quibble over labels. Nor is it to minimize those elements of human dedication and fortitude in suffering that have led some to call *Perkin Warbeck* a tragedy. The play was, after all, entered in the Stationers' Register as a tragedy. The main point, at least to begin with, is merely to remind ourselves that the work has a very large historical component.

Whatever we label the play, moreover, it is well to bear in mind Ribner's analysis of the range of purposes underlying English history plays generally, and especially the "nationalistic glorification of England," the "use of past events as a guide to political behaviour," and the use of the past to flatter, warn, and teach.[5] If history is or ever was a true mirror for magistrates, it follows that history repeats itself. Considering that the present goal is to suggest a Jacobean provenance for *Perkin Warbeck*, furthermore, it may help to recall King James's own advice to his son on the purpose of history: "by reading of Authenticke histories and Chronicles," James counseled, "yee shall learne experience by Theoricke, applying the bypast things to the present estate, *quia nihil nouum sub sole....*"[6]

For most of his history in this play Ford turned to two sources, Francis Bacon and Thomas Gainsford. The latter explained to all readers of *The True and Wonderfull History of Perkin Warbeck* (1618) that he wrote "both for precept, and caution" (A2v). Concerning King Henry, according to Gainsford, "*Heere are manifested his prouidence, wisdome, mightinesse, power, iustice, mercy, preuention, loue, goodnesse, maiesty, &c*" (A4v). This is a potent lot of virtues, and they should be kept in mind for future reference. As Gainsford's title indicates, however, Gainsford's central subject is the cautionary history of Warbeck. Like Gainsford, Bacon also put considerable emphasis on Warbeck, but naturally in a work called *The Historie of the Raigne of King Henry the Seventh* he concentrated more on Henry. Publishing this *Historie* in the year immediately following his own fall from power, he apparently still retained his concern for teaching lessons in political science and also, an inveterate calculator, kept his sights on recouping as much favor as possible from Henry's proud descendant and current successor.

Looking for motives, expressed or implied, in Ford's sources need not lead us into the temptation of deriving Ford's own motivation by association. Lacking a proper time machine, we cannot say for sure why Ford chose to write a history play about Henry VII. We cannot be certain about the nature of his subtext. On the other hand, there is more evidence than we have yet considered. For instance, Ford clearly was neither immune to nor uninformed about what was going on around him at the time he wrote *Fames Memoriall* (on the recent death of the Earl of Devonshire) or *Honor Triumphant* (on a tournament arranged for a visit from the King of Denmark) or *Sir Thomas Overbury's Life and Untimely Death* (entered with the Stationers in the year that Lady Essex's agents were hanged for the murder). Furthermore, he was by no means oblivious to events of his day when he collaborated on *The Witch of Edmonton* and *A Late Murder*, both dramas of the 1620s which are based on current cases.

Another sort of evidence may be relatable to the fact that Bacon himself had perceived and repeatedly noted the drama inherent in the Warbeck phase of Henry's reign. Warbeck, he said, had a "stage-like greatness."[7] Of his story he writes, "It was one of the longest plays of that kind that hath been in memory, and might perhaps have had another end, if he [i.e., Warbeck] had not met with a King both wise, stout, and fortunate" (p. 211). Bacon even observes: "Therefore now (like the end of a play) a great number came upon the stage at once" (p. 201). With this parabolical Baconian approach one might juxtapose a thought-provoking statement made by Gainsford about three years earlier: "how *Perkin Warbeck* ... went forward ... against the house of *Lancaster*, our stages of *London*, have instructed those which cannot read...."[8] No such Warbeck play or plays now survive, unfortunately, instructive or otherwise, but Gainsford surely is correct in stating that they did. Though doubtless the Prologue of *Perkin Warbeck* is also correct in describing history plays as "out of fashion," the bookstalls and stages of the 1620s were not totally without them.[9] Especially provocative is the notice of Samuel Rowley's 1623 *Richard III*, which is now lost but which would have made a fine contemporary complement to Ford's play. So would Shakespeare's *Richard III*, published in 1622. One might add that 1622 saw the separate printings of Shakespeare's *King John* and *1 Henry IV*, as well as Marlowe's *Edward II*. With such a cluster of works in mind, one might suggest that in the early 1620s *Perkin Warbeck* would have been not a totally isolated phenomenon, but one of several works which, for some reason, turned back to explore the subject of English kingship.

CHAPTER TWO

A Show of Kings

Although one might hope that the matter is now beyond dispute, thanks largely to the work of Donald Anderson, it may be advisable to state that the dating and reading offered here are grounded on the observation that *Perkin Warbeck* is centrally concerned with kingship. The play opens with a threatened kingship, then presents the rising and falling arc of the major threat to that kingship, and finally depicts the kingship as firmly established and looking forward, thanks to a wise and skillful king. When it comes time to put a cap on the play, the Epilogue begins, "Here has appeared, though in a several fashion, / The threats of majesty" (ll. 1-2). From beginning to end, furthermore, the play has been redolent with regal language—even in Warbeck's wooing scene, where he is "king" to Katherine. Virtuous Urswick assures Henry, "Your majesty's a wise king, sent from heaven / Protector of the just" (III.i.36-37), and good old Huntly (who must have had a premonition of what James VI would one day write [cf. *Works*, 54, 307]) declares that "kings are earthly gods, there is no meddling / With their anointed bodies" (III.ii.57-58). Warbeck is glorious in his way, to be sure, but ultimately just one of several "threats" or "meddlers" that "majesty" must face. The play is named for Warbeck, but the force which must prevail is the lawful heir, a Henry who is said to be "Divinely strengthened" (I.i.34).

Because of the importance of the theme of kingship in the play, it is significant that John Ford in his other writings provides us with a particularly notable array of statements on Henry's Jacobean heir. In deciding between a Jacobean or Caroline provenance for *Perkin Warbeck*, we should recall that as early as 1606, in *Fames Memoriall*, Ford writes of James as "the monarch of our peace" who "Shall be in after chronicles recited, / In that to heau'ns applause and subiects ease / *England* and *Scotland* he in one vnited" (E1r). Nor is Ford unmindful of James in *Honor Triumphant* (1606), in which he lauds his king as "The mighty ruler of a peacefull land" (E4r). In *A Line of Life* (1620), however, more directly and fully than anywhere else, Ford writes at length of James as a good man, "of whom it may be verified, that he is BONORUM MAXIMUS" and "onely inferior on earth to God...(whose Vicegerent he is)..." (pp. 109, 112-113). James himself could not have put it better.

Before Ford wrote his play, Bacon had already made clear not only the subsuming importance of kingship, but also the great importance of the linkage between Henry VII and James VI and I. Henry's daughter Margaret, whose marriage to James IV is arranged in Ford's play, became the grandmother of Mary Queen of Scots, who was the mother of James VI and I; and by her second marriage Margaret became grandmother of James's father, Henry Stuart, Lord Darnley, who on his father's side was descended from a junior branch of the royal Stuarts and

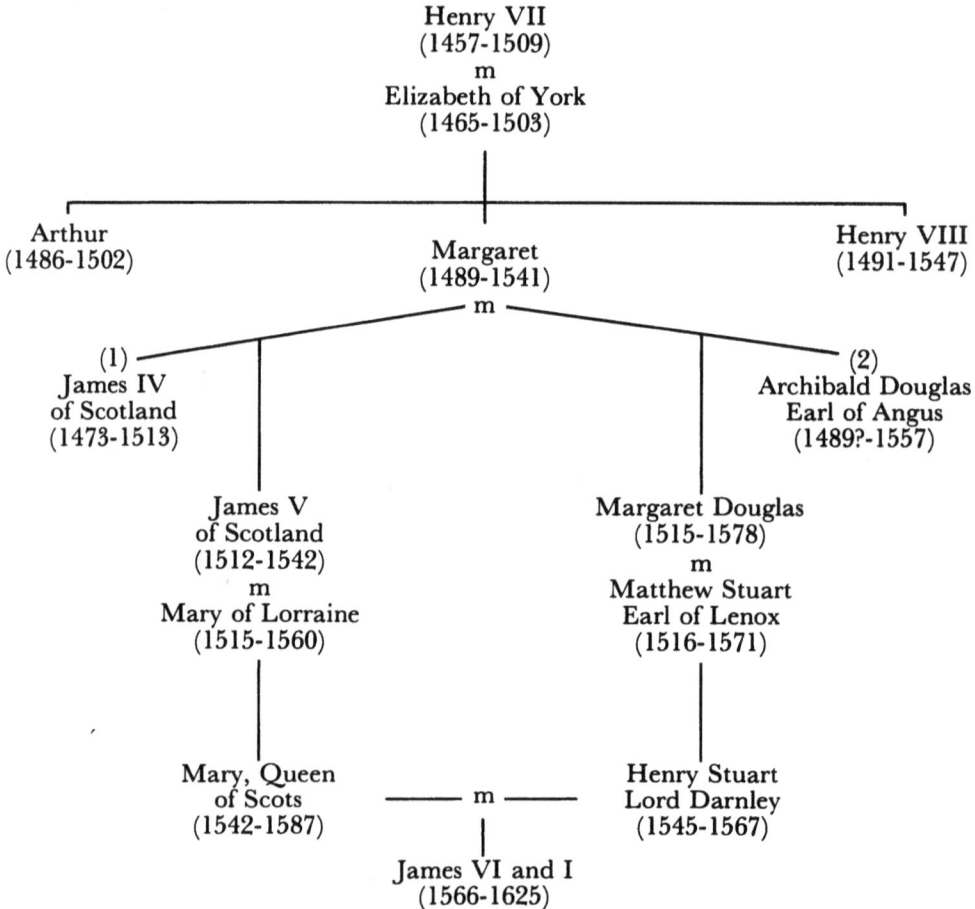

Henry VII
(1457-1509)
m
Elizabeth of York
(1465-1503)

Arthur
(1486-1502)

Margaret
(1489-1541)
m

Henry VIII
(1491-1547)

(1)
James IV
of Scotland
(1473-1513)

(2)
Archibald Douglas
Earl of Angus
(1489?-1557)

James V
of Scotland
(1512-1542)
m
Mary of Lorraine
(1515-1560)

Margaret Douglas
(1515-1578)
m
Matthew Stuart
Earl of Lenox
(1516-1571)

Mary, Queen
of Scots
(1542-1587)

——— m ———

Henry Stuart
Lord Darnley
(1545-1567)

James VI and I
(1566-1625)

Fig. 1.   The descent of James VI and I from Henry VII.

Fig. 2. Henry VII and James VI and I as depicted on the arch commissioned by the Italian merchants for James's entry into London in 1603.

could make a claim to the Scottish throne that was nearly as good as Mary's own (see Fig. 1). This is the way Bacon put it:

> There succeeded . . . to the kingdom of England James the Sixth, then King of Scotland, descended of the same Margaret both by father and mother; so that by a rare event in the pedigrees of Kings, it seemed as if the Divine Providence, to extinguish and take away all note of a stranger, had doubled upon his person, within the circle of one age, the royal blood of England by both parents. This succession drew towards it the eyes of all men; being one of the most memorable accidents that had happened a long time in the Christian world.[1]

When James VI of Scotland came down into England, he did, indeed, bring an extraordinary confluence of lines.

Little wonder is it that the paralleling of Henry with James appeared natural at the beginning of James's reign and that it finally became conventional. In 1603, when James was to be welcomed to London, the arch designed for the Italian merchants depicted Henry presenting a scepter to James as the heir of the Tudor line. (Enlarging the scene here in Fig. 2 has necessitated excising the lower portion of the arch, but it enables us to see better not only the symbolic action and its literal centrality, but also the no-mistakes-wanted labeling of the two kings.)[2] That same year, in his *Panegyrike Congratulatory*, Samuel Daniel spelled out the royal relationship thus:

> The broken frame of this disioynted State,
> Being by the blisse of thy great Grandfather,
> *Henry* the seauenth, restor'd to an estate
> More sound then euer, and farre stedfaster,
> Owes all it hath to him, and in that rate
> Stands bound to thee that art his successor:
> For without him it had not beene begunne,
> And without thee, we had beene now vndone. (A6r)

Just a few years later, in 1610, John Gainsford—the same man who wrote one of Ford's two main sources—chose to publish *The Vision and Discourse of Henry the Seventh*, and although one may not be sure why he did so, the work proved to be in large part a panegyric of James. Among other things, Gainsford has Henry VII observe:

> My great *Grand-sonne* doth hold no other course,
> Then that which vertuous Kings did still intend:
> They alwayes held that Concord was the source
> Of endlesse peace, for this all strife doth end.... (p. 19)

Richard Johnson defined his *Crowne-Garland of Goulden Roses* (1612) as "A PRINCELY SONG / made of the Red Rose and / the White, *royally vnited to /* gether by king *Henry* the seauenth, and / *Elizabeth Plantaginet,* ... / from whom our now / Soueraigne Lord King Iames *linnially / descended*" (title page). The grafting of the red and the white roses recurs in Christopher Brooke's *The Ghost of Richard the Third* (1614):

> ... now *England Chaos* was reduc't to order
> By *God-like Richmond*; whose successiue *Stems*,
> The hand of Time hath Branch't, ...
> Vnto the mem'rie of thrice Royall *Iames*. (L3r)

22

Fig. 3. The entrance to the tomb of Henry VII and James VI and I at Westminster.

As the fallen Lord Chancellor, author of Ford's major source, put it to his king, "I have ... chosen to write the Reign of King Henry the 7th, who was in a sort your forerunner, and whose spirit, as well as his blood, is doubled upon your Majesty."[3] No one could write thus of James's successor.

The paralleling of Henry and James was made easier by James's own attitude. Naming his first son Henry in 1594 may have been an ambiguous signal, since the boy's grandfather was a Henry, but there can be little doubt that the act was also a compliment to the memory of Henry VII. Certainly James valued such parallels. In 1614 he spoke to Parliament on the subject of "Henrye VIIth. my ancestore, from whome I clayme my crowne," reminding the members that King Henry "gave my great-grand-mother the lady Margarate to king James IVth. ..."[4] It was with unmistakable clarity that James spoke to the Star Chamber in 1616 concerning "King *Henry* the Seuenth, from whom, as diuers wayes before, I am lineally descended, and that doubly to this Crowne; and as I am neerest descended of him, so doe I desire to follow him in his best actions" (*Works*, 328). *Nota bene: so doe I desire to follow him in his best actions.* As James had written to his son, "yee shall learne ... by ... applying the bypast things to the present estate. ..."

Last scene of all, when James died, the vault of Henry VII at Westminster Abbey was opened, and both Henry's coffin and that of Elizabeth of York, his queen, were nudged aside to make room for the out-sized coffin of his proud heir. Figs. 3 and 4 here are intended to clarify and emphasize the out-sized dimensions of such a gesture, and to help pique some questions about its meaning. Arthur Stanley, sometime Dean of Westminster, who recorded details of the disinterment of this secret in 1869, recorded also his awareness of some of its powerful and personal implications. At the same time Stanley was struck by the inaccuracy of all printed reports and by the silence of all official accounts regarding the placement of James's body, he also recognized that

> its main interest arose from the insight which it gave into the deep historical instinct which prompted the founder of the Stuart Dynasty, Scotsman and almost foreigner as he was, to ingraft his family and fate on that of the ancient English stock through which he derived his title to the Crown. Apart from his immediate and glorious predecessor—apart from his mother, then lying in her almost empty vault with his eldest son—apart from his two beloved infant daughters—apart from his Queen, who lies alone in her ample vault as if waiting for her husband to fill the vacant space—the first Stuart King who united England and Scotland was laid in the venerable cavern, for such in effect it is, which contained the remains of the first Tudor King who, with

24

Fig. 4.   The coffins of (l. to r.) James VI and I,
Elizabeth of York, and Henry VII.

his Queen, had united the two contending factions of English mediaeval history. The very difficulty of forcing the entrance [to the burial vault], . . . the sanctity of the spot, and the means taken almost as with religious vigilance to guard against further intrusion—show the strength of the determination which carried the first King of Great Britain into the tomb of the last of the Mediaeval Kings, which laid the heir of the Celtic traditions of Scotland by the side of the heir of the Celtic traditions of Wales, the Solomon, as he deemed himself, of his own age, by the side of him whom a wiser than either [namely, Francis Bacon] had already called the Solomon of England.[5]

Moved by what he has seen, Stanley rather pulls out all the stops here. Then again, his various points are well taken and may serve to introduce or reinforce a number of ideas that are significant throughout the present study. Most important at the moment, they help us to see that the paralleling of Henry VII with James VI and I was, for James himself, not merely a matter of public image, of royal stance, but also a private, personal matter that lay in his heart's deepest core.

Three Royal Matches

To structure our pursuit of some of these subjects, let us consider the three marriages which contributed so greatly to the consolidation of Henry VII's power. And be it noted that none of the three brides or wives concerned is brought to Ford's stage—probably because in each case the individual woman is of far less importance than what her match means.

Since his claim to the English throne was not beyond question, Henry VII took steps after his victory at Bosworth (August, 1485) to have himself crowned (October, 1485), then to consolidate his powers in miscellaneous official ways, and only then—it was still done quickly enough—to strengthen the position of his family yet further by marrying Elizabeth of York (January, 1486), eldest daughter of Edward IV. "By reason of whiche mariage," wrote Edward Hall, "peace was thought to discende oute of heauen into England, consideryng that the lynes of Lancastre & Yorke . . . were now . . . connexed together, of whose twoo bodyes one heyre might succede, which after their tyme should peaceably rule and enioye the whole monarchy and realme of England."[1] In I.i of Ford's play, consequently, we find Daubeney using the following terms to support Henry's claim that he rules by "royal birthright" (l. 9): "For Edward's daughter is king Henry's queen— / A blessed union, and a lasting blessing / For this poor panting island . . ." (ll. 38-40). All of the opening speeches in the play, it might be added, contribute in some way to affirm Henry's legitimacy or to decry the "pageant majesty" (I.i.3) that threatens it. Here, already, is the major antagonism that fuels the play.

In the same year as the union by marriage of Lancaster and York, Elizabeth presented Henry with a son. The name chosen for the infant was "Arthur," which was meant to be a verbal reminder of the link between this family and its supposed ancient British royal ancestors. Perceiving, furthermore, that a strategic second royal match would be one of the most efficient ways for the Tudors to gain equal standing among the great contemporary ruling houses of Europe, Henry soon approached Ferdinand and Isabella regarding a marriage between young Prince Arthur and the *infanta* Katherine of Aragon. In *Perkin Warbeck* Ford changes history a bit in this matter so as to enhance England's position, having Hialas say, "The King of Spain resolves a marriage / For Katherine his daughter, with Prince Arthur" (IV.iii.8-9). Partly because of the age of the children, in any case, and partly for political reasons, negotiations stretched on for years. In the words of Bacon, Henry and the Catholic Kings,

> being Princes of great policy and profound judgment, stood a great time looking one upon another's fortunes, how they would go; knowing well that in the mean time the very treaty itself gave abroad in the world a reputation of a strait conjunction and amity between them, which served on both sides to many purposes that their several affairs required, and yet they continued still free. (pp. 217-218)

Unfortunately, only a few months after the marriage took place in 1501, the fifteen-year-old husband was dead. The rest of the story concerns us less, however, than the fact that this Prince of Wales had been the focal figure in negotiations for a Spanish match throughout most of the decade of the 1490s.

The third marriage to consider is that which in 1503 intertwined the thistle and the rose by the simple means of marrying Margaret, daughter of Henry and Elizabeth, to James IV of Scotland. Here is that great-grandmother on whom James's pedigree hung so heavily. Ford has the Spanish ambassador explain that to the peaceful "union" of Scotland and England "The good of both the church and commonwealth / Invite 'ee" (IV.iii.14, 15-16). But the highest words of all are left for the Bishop of Durham—Henry's mainstay in the first and last scenes:

> To this unity, a mystery
> Of providence points out a greater blessing
> For both these nations than our human reason
> Can search into. King Henry hath a daughter,
> The princess Margaret; I need not urge
> What honour, what felicity can follow.... (IV.iii.16-21)

The language is decidedly forward-looking, but it is also non-specific, so one may only suggest that from Ford's point of view the "greater blessing" is less likely to have been Margaret's immediate offspring than James VI and I himself, monarch over Scotland and England, and the living symbol of their union. Any offspring of James naturally would carry on the merged tradition, of course, but only in a dilute solution: Charles's blood came half from a Danish princess, and the mother of that princess, in turn, was a daughter of the Duke of Mecklenburg. The referent of "a greater blessing" sounds like James himself and the wonders he could bring—perhaps including splendid successors. One of the things the passage does *not* sound like is criticism of King Charles's botched foreign policy.

CHAPTER FOUR

One Happy Britannia

At the time James VI and I was born, his mother Mary said, "This is the son whom I hope shall first unite the two kingdoms of Scotland and England."[1] James never lost sight of this hope. Several years before he came to England he advised Prince Henry in his *Basilikon Doron* (1599) that

> the long warres and many bloodie battels betwixt these two countreys, bred naturall and hereditarie hatred in euery of them, against the other: the vniting and welding of them hereafter in one, by all sort of friendship, commerce, and alliance, wil by the contrary produce and maintaine a naturall and inseparable vnitie of loue amongst them. (*Works*, 51)

A few years later, after it had become clear to Englishmen that James really was deeply committed to the concept of concord, the author of *Perkin Warbeck* wrote in *Fames Memoriall* that

> . . . *Iames* the monarch of our peace,
> Shall be in after chronicles recited,
> In that, to heau'ns applause and subiects ease
> *England* and *Scotland* he in one vnited,
> A sight with which true *Britains* were delighted. . . . (E1r)

Given the author and the subject of our play, these are words worth reading twice.

In 1603, at the beginning of his reign, James had confidently explained his plan for "the Vnion of two ancient and famous Kingdomes" (*Works*, 271), and he himself drafted the document intended to get the merger going. England and Scotland were to be one in state, law, and church. There was even to be a new gold coin called a "unity." To a degree never inherited by Charles, James advocated and advanced the union in every way he could, even having himself proclaimed King of Great Britain when Parliament would not approve of the title. Time and again his efforts were thwarted, however, by Englishmen who feared a diminution of their wealth and power, and by Scots who may have feared most for the contamination of their kirk. Still, James never let go. The passing years showed him that, despite certain gains now and then,

Fig. 5. *The Union of England and Scotland* as painted by Rubens for the
Banqueting House Ceiling at Whitehall.

there was to be no union in his time, but when he died, the flag symbolizing the Union of the Two Crosses of England and Scotland was carried at his funeral, and engraved on the copper plate that was soldered to his leaden coffin were the words "Depositum Augustissimi Principis Jacobi Primi, Magnae Britanniae, Franciae et Hiberniae Regis...."[2] Still later, Charles had Rubens paint on the Banqueting House ceiling at Whitehall a panel which depicts James crowned and wearing state robes, pointing his scepter at a naked child, above whose head a Minerva-like figure (some call her Britannia) wisely binds together two crowns, one held by England, the other by Scotland (see Fig. 5).[3]

The essentially Jacobean theme of national union naturally crops up in various kinds of writing. Sir William Cornwallis, in his *Miraculous and Happie Union of England and Scotland* (1604), gave James's personal relationship with each of these kingdoms as a reason for his commitment to both: "since he is King of both, he is father of both, and (being equally charged by the King of Kings with both) owing vnto both one duty, he will giue vnto both one affection" (B3v). In 1603 Daniel had already exclaimed prematurely in his *Panegyrike*, "Now thou art all great *Brittaine*, and no more, / No Scot, no English now, nor no debate..." (A1r). In his first masque (1605) Jonson made considerable to-do over the search for a "blessèd isle" whose name ends in "-tania," coming finally to "Britannia, whose new name makes all tongues sing."[4] In *The Triumphes of Reunited Britania*, Anthony Munday that same year helped to bolster the historical implications of the name by writing of

> the blessed marriage *of Margaret*, eldest daughter to king *Henrie* the seauenth, to *Iames* the fourth king of *Scotland*, of whom our second *Brute* (Royall king *Iames*) is truely and rightfully descended: by whose happy comming to the Crowne, *England*, *Wales*, & *Scotland*, by the first *Brute* seuered and diuided, is in our second *Brute* re-united, and made one happy *Brittania* again....
>
> (B1v-B2r)

In his fifth "Epigram" Jonson wrote of the union of the two countries as a marriage, and in *Hymenaei* (1607) he used the subject of marital union as an excuse for writing an apostrophe to the Union that may have meant most to James: "Long may his union find increase / As he to ours hath deigned his peace" (ll. 387-388). It was, after all, a metaphor that James specifically approved.[5]

With even so small a handful of examples, perhaps one is better able to interpret the full title of Thomas Gainsford's previously cited pamphlet,

The Visions and Discourse of Henry the Seventh. Concerning the Unitie of Great Brittaine. In the period proposed here for Ford's *Perkin Warbeck*, Tom Tell Troath scoffed, "They make a mock of your word Great Brittaine,"[6] but when we turn to the play itself we should pause to ponder the implications of the fact that the setting of this work is specified to be not England and Scotland but, rather grandly, "*The Continent of Great Britayne*" (A1v).

Within the play, in fact, and emphasizing the subject of British unification still further, Ford presents the joining of England and Scotland as nothing less than the capstone to universal peace. Through a friendly outside observer, the Spanish envoy Hialas, we are informed that

> France, Spain, and Germany combine a league
> Of amity with England; nothing wants
> For settling peace through Christendom but love
> Between the British monarchs, James and Henry.
> (IV.iii.1-4)

It was all a many-splendored dream that one might suppose to lie beyond mere human achievement, of course, but nevertheless, a century and a quarter later, it was the dream of Ford's own king.

CHAPTER FIVE

Games at Chess

Henry VII's second great marriage match, that of Arthur, Prince of Wales, to a Spanish princess, was followed not only by the marriage of Arthur's widow, Katherine, to Prince Henry and by the betrothal of Princess Mary to Charles, Prince of Castile (later Charles V), and still later by the marriage of Queen Mary (daughter of Henry VIII) to her cousin Philip of Spain, but also by the betrothal of Charles, son of James VI and I, to the Spanish *infanta* Maria, daughter of Philip III and Margaret of Austria. For about seven months in 1623 Charles was in Spain to negotiate for the match in person, thereby arousing a wide spectrum of strong feelings among the English people. But soon after his safe return, the spectrum shrank drastically. Charles's return, says Garrett Mattingly, "set off the fiercest wave of anti-Catholic and anti-Spanish feeling which England had seen since Armada Days."[1]

Taking Bacon's 1622 *Historie* as our *terminus a quo* for Ford's play, then, and hypothesizing that the conflagration of passions following this aborted Spanish Match might possibly constitute a *terminus ad quem*, let us consider some more facts in the case. In his *Basilikon Doron* James had warned Prince Henry against *"the inconuenients that were like to ensew, incase he should marry any that be of a different profession in Religion from him"* (*Works*, 8), but in later years James thought more in terms of unifying not only Englishman and Scot, but also Protestant and Catholic. The matter is complex, but for over a decade at the close of his life (comparable, one might argue, to the 1490s in Henry VII's reign), James negotiated to marry an English prince to a Spanish princess. In a 1621 pamphlet called *Vox Spiritus* the busy Thomas Gainsford chose to use the ghost of Sir Walter Raleigh—executed by James in 1618 more or less upon pressure from Spain—to cry out against the dangers of dealing with Spain. Thomas Scott, meanwhile, had begun to pour forth what would finally prove to be a veritable stream of well-informed anti-Spanish invective. English hatred and fear discovered that a possible anagram for the Spanish ambassador's name was "Roman dog." And in Parliament in November of 1621, man after man arose to argue the need for enforcing the laws against recusants and for going to war with Spain.

While much evidence of this sort has been garnered and made the common currency of our conversation about the period, we have almost lost sight of the Englishmen to whom the Spanish Ambassador referred as the *bien intenciados*.[2] Here, then, is a smattering of counter-evidence. Merely noting Thomas Shelton's landmark translation of *Don Quixote* in 1620, and moving to 1622, we find James Wadsworth's translation from César Oudin called *A Grammar Spanish and English*. Someone must have felt a need for such books, certainly including Prince Charles, who started taking Spanish lessons that year, and Thomas, Lord Howard, Earl of Surrey (there is an earlier Surrey in Ford's play) and Arundel, to whom *A Grammar* was dedicated. The year 1622 brought forth also *The Spanish Curate*, *The Sea Voyage*, and *The Prophetess*, all by Fletcher and Massinger and all based on Spanish writings, as were Chapman's *Chabot* and Middleton and Rowley's *Changeling*, the latter with a notable insistence on its Spanish setting.[3] Dating dramas of the period is no easy matter, of course, but it appears that 1622 saw the initial appearance of more English plays based on Spanish sources than did any other single year before the Restoration. Nor is this all one may say. It is now many years since attention was first called to the extraordinary fact that of the seven books of fiction now known to have been published in 1622, three were from the Spanish.[4] *Gerardo the Unfortunate Spaniard*, translated by Leonard Digges from the work of Gonzalo de Céspedes y Meneses, appeared not only as itself, so to speak, but also provided Middleton and Rowley with some of the main plot for *The Changeling*. Juan de Luna, a Spanish teacher in London, wrote an original Spanish story and then Englished it (or saw it Englished) as *The Pursuit of the Historie of Lazarillo de Tormez*. Whoever he was, the translator dedicated his efforts to the children of the Earl of Derby (there is kindly reference to an earlier Derby in Ford's play), and he included a letter to Derby's son-in-law Robert Carr of Ancram of the "Camara Priuada," notable at the time for being "gran Tesorero de . . . su *Alteça el Principe de Galles*" (A4r). Most impressive of all, however (Ben Jonson wished he himself might claim the book), James Mabbe translated from Mateo Alemán a work he called *The Rogue: or The Life of Guzman de Alfarache*—a major fiction to which scholars of English have still not paid adequate attention.

Similar Spanish cross-currents—never stronger in English history, either earlier or later—continue into 1623. In February Dr. Joseph Meade reported on the entertainment at Cambridge for the ambassadors from Madrid and Brussels: the college "Orators fathered the foundation of our University upon the Spanyards out of the old legend of

A

Gamᵉ at Chæss as it was Acted nine days to gether at the Globe

The Black-House | on the banks side | The White-House.

Black Q: Black K: White K: White Q:

Black D: White D:

Fatte Bishop White B:

the Fatte Bishop   the Black Knight   the White Knight

A letter from his Holynes

Keepe ý distance

Chess

Fig. 6.   The title page of Middleton's *A Game at Chaess* (1625), with the Gondomar-like Black Knight at bottom center.

36

Cantaber,—how happie we were not only to see them here, but should be to have the Spanish blood come hither...."⁵ James Mabbe (who signed himself with the punning name "Don Diego Puede-Ser") brought forth another edition of *The Rogue*, in which he included a dedication in Spanish to "DON IVAN ESTRANGWAYES," "gentilhombre de la Camara de Su Serenissima Magesdad de la gran Bretaña." And the anonymous translator who in 1621 had offered the public his version of *The Pilgrime of Casteele*, based on a long narrative by Lope de Vega, now in 1623 saw his work issued twice more. The year 1623 also saw timely language aids. Richard Perceval dedicated *A Dictionary in Spanish and English* to his forerunner John Minsheu, and Juan de Luna (the *Lazarillo* continuator) published *A Short and Compendious Aid for to Learne to Read, Write, Pronounce and Speake the Spanish Tongue*. Meanwhile, someone thought it worthwhile to publish a new edition of *The Spanish Tragedy*, and Middleton and Rowley, with a Spanish play to their credit from the previous year, now saw the licensing of their *Spanish Gipsy*. Brittin writes of this work:

> The play was first acted, and was probably composed, while Prince Charles and the Duke of Buckingham were in Spain; they had left England on February 18, 1623. The consequent topical interest of the play perhaps occasioned a need for haste in preparing for it, and the necessity of haste may have caused Middleton and Rowley to ask another writer for his help.... The political situation and the interest of the British public in Spain during the early summer of 1623 enhance the possibility that John Ford was invited to collaborate on *The Spanish Gipsy*.⁶

One might add two points: first, that both plots of *The Spanish Gipsy* are lifted from stories told in Cervantes' *Novelas ejemplares*; and, second, that it would not have been the first time Ford had engaged in a timely, topical work.

Since timeliness seems to be one key to Middleton and Rowley's joint efforts, it is striking that in 1624, the very next year, Middleton wrote and Rowley starred in *A Game at Chesse*, famed now for achieving a nineday run on the stage and for being the most propagandistic of all Jacobean plays, and—a major point here—noteworthy for its white-vs.-black, anti-Spanish virulence. The play's personal attack on Gondomar, potent enough in the script itself, was intensified still more if it is true, as report had it, that the player taking the role of the Black Knight was furnished with one of the ambassador's own cast-off suits. (One of the 1625 title pages which pictures the black-suited Black Knight is reproduced here as Fig. 6.) The White King, obviously suggestive of James, is depicted in the play as not only exultant over the safe return home of the

White Knight, obviously Charles, but as driving the hapless Black King and Queen into hell. (To the left of the Black Knight in the title-page picture one may see the hell-mouth-like bag which eventually serves as a receptacle for all on the Black side.) Clearly the great change in Middleton and Rowley's public stance toward Spain between 1623 and 1624 is worth a moment or two of reflection.

The chorus of history has dealt so sternly with the Jacobean Spanish Match that it is difficult now to recall why some men ever viewed it positively. There were reasons: the acquisition of "a great Kings daughter," "much mony" (an enormous dowry of £600,000), "safety," "continuance of trade," "the bridling of the overgrowing greatnes of the States" (of the Low Countries), and a belief that "the Subiects of Spain will not be ... [so] burthensome to England being more remote, as those of France would be...."[7] In *The Spanish-English Rose or The English-Spanish Pomgranet*, Michael duVal signs himself *"in Heart and* AFFECTION *an* ENGLISH-SPANIARD" (A3v-A4r), and he asks his countrymen, "But grant that *Spaniards* were sometimes your Aduersaries and *Enemies.* / Shall there *therefore*, neuer be an end of Enmity?" (p. 54). Fig. 7 translates some of DuVal's ideas into visual terms, driving home in striking fashion the strong religious element involved in the Match. Bishop Goodman, in closing his own comments on the subject, writes that King James, "conceiving it to be most fit to match with the Spaniard, as Henry the Seventh, that wise, great prince did; stood still constant and resolute in his first intention."[8]

Helping to make the business attractive to James were the great diplomatic and social skills of Diego Sarmiento de Acuña, Conde de Gondomar, Spain's Ambassador to England (1613-1618; 1620-1622), who privately believed that "At any price ... the friendship of James must be secured. With that, everything would be possible, even the reduction of England to the Catholic church."[9] When Gondomar returned to England in March, 1620, for his second stint, James told him that he wished to marry the English prince to no one except the *infanta*, and that he desired no alliance but with Spain. The following summer, even after a Spanish army had invaded the Palatinate, the home of James's daughter, now Queen of Bohemia, James continued to hold firm, finally commanding that no member of the Commons should "presume to meddle with any thing concerning our government or mysteries of state" or "speak of our dearest son's match with the daughter of Spain...."[10]

The period beginning in 1621 and ending in early 1624 is of sufficient

CASTRA HÆC FIRMANTIA SCEPTRA.

SIC OMNIA VNVM

MANET VLTIMA CÆLO | ET SOLO ET POLO

HVNQVAM MARCESCO | CORDA REVINCIT AMOR | MEDICABILE SEMPER

ROSA HISPANI——ANGLICA
SEV
MALVM PVNICVM ANGL' HISPANICVM·

DOMINI BENEDICTIO DITAT

Fig. 7   The Spanish Match as represented in DuVal's
The Spanish-English Rose (1623?).

consequence to us to deserve a brief chronological sketch. When Philip III died in March, 1621, John Digby, Lord Bristol, was sent to Madrid under the guise of congratulating Philip IV on his accession, but mainly to commence new negotiations for a Spanish marriage. And in April, Digby "was told that whatever the late sovereign might have said, Philip IV. was most anxious to go on vigorously with the marriage treaty."[11] The possibility of a royal union seemed greater than ever. In July, Gondomar was "so affable and familiar that... with his whole train he went to a common play at the Fortune in Golding Lane, and the players (not to be overcome with courtesy) made him a banquet when the play was done[,] in the garden adjoining."[12] In August, Ben Jonson had Lord Feilding, Buckingham's brother-in-law, refer to Philip IV and the *infanta* in his jocular gypsy masque: "She is sister of a star, / One the noblest now that are, / Bright Hesper..." (ll. 355-357).

In 1622 James pressed hard for the marriage. Proposed articles for the marriage treaty had been sent to Spain long before, but the Pope did not care to grant easy approval. Meanwhile, Gondomar's term of duty came to an end (to the joy of many Englishmen), and his successor, Don Carlos de Coloma, was liked rather better. Gondomar still continued to keep an eye on English matters, however, and James's favorite, Buckingham, wrote to him thus: "As for the news from hence, I can in a word assure you that they are in all points as your heart could wish. For here is a king, a prince, and a faithful friend and servant unto you, besides a number of your other good friends that long so much for the happy accomplishment of this match, as every day seems a year unto us. ...."[13] That winter the English began to ready a fleet to fetch the *infanta* home.

This is the background for Charles's and Buckingham's sudden jaunt to Spain, made to hasten and insure the marriage. Traveling incognito (one of them dropped his false beard at Gravesend), they arrived in Madrid in early March, 1623, at which time Charles was given a royal welcome and greeted everywhere by the shout, "Viva el Principe de Galles!"[14] Buckingham wrote to James about his Spanish "daughter," and back in England the matrimonial contract was signed and the Spanish Ambassador laid the foundation stone for the *infanta*'s new chapel. James asked a beloved old friend, the Duke of Richmond, to arrange for welcoming "shews and Pageants, to which purpose Inigo Jones and [Edward] Allen the old Player went along...." The *infanta* began to be styled "Princesa de Inglaterra," and James, writing a letter to her, signed himself "Vostre tresaffectionné Père."[15]

Nevertheless, and despite the hopes and hoopla, the project for many reasons began to crumble. Finally, on 5 October 1623, Charles and Buckingham landed at Portsmouth *sans infanta*. Bells rang, bonfires blazed, and St. Paul's resounded with the joyous words, "Israel came out of Egypt, and the House of Jacob from among the barbarous people." As late as 11 November, young Maria herself was said to be still proceeding cheerfully to learn English (one may doubt the adverb), but already it was too late for a play like *Perkin Warbeck*. In his *Neptune* masque, originally scheduled for production in January, 1624, Jonson writes of young Albion going forth into Celtiberia. He touches on the preceding year's fears for the youth ("How near our general joy was to be lost"), and he observes that that near loss is but one of the things to "make / The present gladness greater" (ll. 104, 106). On 25 March James issued a declaration breaking off England's treaty with Spain. Clearly the climate was now right for Middleton's *Game at Chesse* (licensed 12 June 1624). As for Charles, he expressed himself most eloquently, perhaps, by giving one of his footmen the golden bowl that had been presented to him by the Queen of Spain. On 27 March 1625 he succeeded James as king, and on May Day that year he was married by proxy at Notre Dame, Paris, to a sister of the King of France.

Against such a backdrop we can hope to understand better Ford's very positive handling of the Spanish Match at the court of Henry VII. The nuptial arrangements in the play are effected mainly through the skilled offices of the Spanish ambassador, who is identified as a Castilian in the second line of his first scene (III.iii). Pedro Hialas has come to serve as "an ambassador / To Scotland, for a peace between our kingdoms" (III.iii.16-17). In Ford's words, he is sent to express "A policy of love" (l. 18). As soon as he departs from the scene, however (and Henry says, "A hearty love go with you" [l. 38]), we learn more specifically that the unification and peace for which Hialas strives—by commission of the admirable Ferdinand—embraces a royal marriage between England and Spain. All told, Hialas appears in only three of the play's eighteen scenes, and he speaks a total of only about thirty lines, but he is the vital link between England and Scotland, on the one hand, and between England and Spain on the other. This fine Spaniard, a man of "right modest gravity" (III.iii.46)—and therefore a character who differs greatly and provocatively from the stereotypical Spaniard depicted in most Renaissance English writings—is a potent and beneficent force for peace and unity.[16]

The final stage picture in the play, in fact what amounts to a striking ceremonial *tableau vivant* in the last scene, is especially helpful for

41

clarifying Hialas's function not just as a character but even more as a symbol. The scene as a whole is a long one that is structured as a sequence of character groupings, but it postpones King Henry's return to the stage until the final moments, and then places him in a physical configuration that echoes and reminds us of the formalized stage management at the opening of the play. The first time we ever see Henry, he is standing with the dependable Durham on one side and (as we soon learn) the traitorous Stanley on the other. In the beginning, as the text makes clear, the English throne is in need of strengthening. It must be made safe from "unthankful beasts" and "false ... pageant majesty" (I.i.80, 2-3). Then at the close of the play we have a character triad once more. The focus emphatically remains on Henry, naturally, and again we have Durham—Durham, whom we previously have heard extolling "peace, the crowning of an empire" (IV.i.17). And this time we have on Henry's other side the Spaniard Hialas. Although he speaks not a word, Hialas is visually valuable along with Durham because these two are the co-negotiators of Henry's greatest and most recent diplomatic achievement. In case we have any doubt about how to respond to Ford's placement of Hialas in this symbolic picture, Bacon can help us resolve them: "Peter Hialas ... surely ... was the forerunner of the good hap that we enjoy at this day: for his ambassage set the truce between England and Scotland; the truce drew on the peace; the peace the marriage; and the marriage the union of the kingdoms ..." (p. 195). Strange, indeed, would it be if Ford were to create such a Spaniard, such a stage picture, after Charles became king.[17]

CHAPTER SIX

Triumphs of Peace

Ford's theme of unity and peace in this play is particularly Jacobean—and, forerunning and reinforcing that, Henrician. Gainsford reports specifically that Henry VII boasted "of the character of Prince of peace."[1] William Slatyer, who published his *History of Great Britanie* in 1621, not only made use of the now-familiar parallel of Henry and James, but specified that Henry had "Concluded such perpetuall peace, / As after ages all should blesse . . ." (p. 269). And Bacon recorded that "He preferred always to love and seek peace; and it was his usual preface in his treaties, that when Christ came into the world peace was sung, and when he went out of the world peace was bequeathed" (p. 240). Little wonder, then, that Ford's Henry exclaims, "Good fate, speak peace to Henry!" (III.i.42).

On the other hand, James himself worked harder than any other English king in history to claim the title of *Rex Pacificus*. In 1603 he assured his first Parliament that

> The first . . . of these blessings, which God hath ioyntly with my Person sent vnto you, is outward Peace: that is, peace abroad with all forreine neighbours. . . . And . . . the second great blessing that God hath with my Person sent vnto you, is Peace within, and that in a double forme. First, by my descent lineally out of the loynes of *Henry* the seuenth, is reunited and confirmed in mee the Vnion of the two Princely Roses of the two Houses of Lancaster and Yorke. . . . But the Vnion of these two princely Houses, is nothing comparable to the Vnion of two ancient and famous Kingdomes, which is the other inward Peace annexed to my Person. . . . (*Works*, 270-271)

In the following year, still at the opening of his reign, he managed to achieve peace with Spain, England's greatest foe. For a motto he took the seventh Beatitude, "Beati pacifici," which is an important element in (among other places) the engraving used as a frontispiece in his own volume of *Workes* (1616; see Fig. 8). As Parry observes, "the figure of Peace became the most predictable and over-employed goddess in the Jacobean pantheon" (p. 18). And the fact that James really did manage to maintain peace encouraged countless writers of various sorts to take up the theme.

Fig. 8   James VI and I with his motto "Beati pacifici," from the Van de Passe
frontispiece in James's *Workes* (1616).

To refine this last point briefly, let us consider a few citations from late in the reign. In 1618 a quarto pamphlet called *The Peace-Maker: or, Great Brittaines Blessing*—the very title of which echoes James's first speech to Parliament—was anonymous, but provided with a preface that suggests royal backing: "To all Our true-louing, and Peace-embracing Subiects" (A3r). The London pageant for 1620 was John Squire's *Triumphs of Peace*, in which Peace, wearing a "robe... of white taffaty, limm'd with the map of England," came down from her celestial home to make England happy.[2] In 1622 John Taylor the Water Poet addressed James as "The Prince of Peace, / The blest *Concorder* that made wars to cease...."[3] Of course there were also voices to complain that unlimited peace was a limited blessing, but in 1623, perhaps the final year of major interest for this study, we find Ben Jonson speaking out yet again, now in *Time Vindicated*, saying that James "studies only ways of good / To keep soft Peace in breath" (ll. 426-427). Middleton's *Triumphs of Integrity* that same year displayed James's motto of "Beati pacifici" in "faire great Letters" and spoke of "*that Royall Peace-maker, our King*" (B4v). Sir John Stradling produced his interminable anatomy of peace entitled *Beati Pacifici: A Divine Poem Written to the Kings Most Excellent Maiestie*, which, like Bacon's *Historie*, previously had been "Perused by his Maiesty" (title page). And James himself pointed out to Parliament that he had been "all the days of my life, a peaceable king," rather proudly reminding the members that "I... have had the honour, in my titles and impresses, to be s[t]iled '*Rex Pacificus.*'"[4]

Such details help to emphasize that any compliments Ford expresses or implies about Henry VII as a peace-maker in *Perkin Warbeck* are likely to be compliments also to Henry's self-avowed imitator, James. In his 1620 *Line of Life*, Ford himself writes of his monarch as "IAMES THE PEACEABLE" (p. 111). It is therefore not merely interesting but also useful to know that according to Anderson's reckoning, the word "peace" occurs in the play an extraordinary twenty-two times.[5] Peace, says Durham, is "the crowning of an empire" (IV.i.17). As a matter of historical fact, James managed to maintain peace for over twenty years after that spring of 1603 when he first came down from Scotland.

Charles's reign was different from the very start. At Charles's coronation, as at James's, there was no procession, ostensibly because of the plague but actually, it was thought, because Charles wished to save money for a Spanish war. Whatever his motive was, Charles certainly sent Englishmen off to fight a maritime war against Spain in the very year that James died. "Our honor is ruined, our ships are sunk, our men

45

perished," Sir John Eliot told the Commons.[6] In the following year a dispute over shipping precipitated war with France. The year after that, the expedition that Charles sent to the Isle of Rhé had to endure one of the most humiliating defeats in the history of England. Buckingham brought back only about three thousand of the eight thousand men he had taken. It is also true that after several years of military blundering, Charles made peace with France (1629) and Spain (1630), and after that, that his pursuit of a policy of neutrality enabled England to entertain what has been called "the Caroline myth of Peace."[7] Hence one should note that *Perkin Warbeck*, with its emphasis on peace, was finally published in the same year that saw Shirley's *Triumph of Peace* and Carew's *Coelum Britannicum*. But even these works proved to be somewhat ambivalent in their praise.[8] Furthermore, although Charles's rather isolated, self-sufficing court managed to set aside military conflict for a time, it never looked far enough beyond its own confines to grasp the large-scale ideal of peace on which James had set his sights and to which he remained faithful, in his fashion, from the beginning of his reign to the end.

CHAPTER SEVEN

Honorable Scots

In deciding to dramatize the story of Perkin Warbeck, Ford could easily
follow his monarch's own lead by paralleling Henry's reign with
James's, but in doing so he had to deal also with the concomitant
challenge of writing acceptably about James's somewhat problematic
royal Scottish forebear, James IV. Things must be so arranged that
neither king in the drama come off badly. The solution, present in the
play as we have it, is to show James IV as immature but learning, and to
use Warbeck's supporters as a sort of lightning rod for criticism. In life,
there appear to have been three kinds of reasons for James IV to have
taken up Warbeck. First, the group that had overthrown James's father
did so in part because they thought him too friendly with Henry VII, so
when the fifteen-year-old James IV came to the throne, badly jolted by
his father's murder (1488), it was as head of the anti-English party.
Considering everything, the arrival of "Duke Richard" in Scotland
(1495) might well have been viewed by James as the acquisition of a
good new weapon for the royal Scottish arsenal. Second, if Warbeck
were to prove successful in his bid for the English throne, James stood to
receive 100,000 marks and even some English lands. Third, James was
young, naive, impetuous, and impressionable. Obviously Ford chose to
explore this third area, and the result is that whereas in his Henry VII we
have a mature, well-seasoned monarch, we have in James IV an
admirable king-in-the making, on the road to wisdom, but still capable
of committing errors. King Henry, who may by definition be trusted to
say the right thing, says, "A' studies to be wise betimes..." (V.ii.19).
   Tracing the role of the Scottish king, who actually marches against
England in the play, helps one to see Ford's artfulness. When we meet
him, James is savoring "court delights" and cheerfully anticipating
"high attempts of honour" (II.i.111, 113)—matters not altogether
scorned by John Ford, author of *Honor Triumphant*, whose sometime
motto, an anagram of his name, was "Fide Honor." Ford does what he
can to soften James's responsibility for wrongdoing and at the same time
tell the story. When James and Warbeck are both on the march against
Henry, for instance, the English king refers to "Our competitor [not

47

"competitors"] / The Flemish counterfeit, with James of Scotland" (III.i.29-30). Warbeck is the enemy, James simply "with" him. When Durham addresses James at Norham, it is as "Warlike king of Scotland" and "Courageous prince," epithets that define without damning (III.iv.10, 14). "So like a king a' speaks," exclaims England's fine courtier Surrey (IV.i.36), impressed by James's "unfellowed grace" (IV.i.30). James is allowed a rash, low moment in which he gives orders to "Forage through / The country; spare no prey of life or goods" (III.iv.54-55), but a major and probably well-calculated effect of this speech is to bring into startling relief the pretender's response: "Spare, spare, my dear, dear England!" (III.iv.67). In any event, the moment is qualified almost immediately by James's own "brave defiance / For single combat" with Surrey (III.iv.99-100), which may be his noblest moment of all. Says Oxford, "The Scottish king showed more than common bravery / In proffer of a combat hand to hand . . ." (IV.iv.10-11). And we have already heard the astute Hialas, a man of yet another nation, tell him, "You are a just king" (IV.iii.49). Furthermore, when we see James enter to play his last scene (IV.iii), he appears as the central figure in a deictic triad that parallels (it both echoes and prefigures) those with which, as we have noted, the more important figure of Henry opens and closes the play. The Scottish king comes on with the Englishman Durham on one side and the Spaniard Hialas on the other—in other words, with the two chief negotiators commissioned to bring peace to Great Britain, the two men who, in a significant modulation, appear once again with Henry at the end.

As one analyzes Ford's craftsmanship, one cannot but be struck also by the attention he gives to all his Scots. After the opening scene, in which he introduces seven speaking English characters, he takes us to Scotland and works with only four speaking Scots, and yet these four share about a third more dialogue. Fewer characters are developed at greater leisure and length. In fact, if we consider the play as a whole, we find that following the two major roles, those of Henry and Warbeck, the next three largest are those of Huntly, James, and Katherine. Moreover, the "supporting" Scots are all good characters. This is the more striking when one recalls how often in real life the English subjects of James VI and I denigrated his Scottish ones—"the sonnes of the locusts and daughters of the hors[e]leach."[1] As Ford's editor Gifford observed long ago, "No drama that I am acquainted with, offers four such admirable characters as Huntley and his daughter, the lady Jane, and Dalyell."[2] Katherine is, as Warbeck says, a "Great miracle of constancy!" and "a

48

pattern / For every virtuous wife..." (V.iii.89, 93-94), and Katherine calls Dalyell a "Rare unexampled pattern of a friend!" (IV.v.17). What is Ford attempting to achieve by means of these fine Scots? Arthur L. and M. K. Kistner observed some years ago that Ford was clearly interested in the possibilities that these characters present for winning sympathy for Warbeck.[3] That is a sound observation, but it is true also that if one were a Jacobean trying to write a play whose resolution involved the merger of England and Scotland, one would do well to have some virtuous Scots on hand.

In order to convey something of the idealized essence of the Scots, Ford the craftsman turns again to formalizing, triadic stage iconography. At the point where Huntly, despite his quirky, gruff exterior, expresses his approval of Dalyell's suit to Katherine, Ford writes lines for the old father that inevitably propel the three players performing these roles into visual symbolism. Addressing both Katherine and Dalyell, Huntly says,

> Then hear me, Kate.
> Keep you on that hand of her; I on this:
> Thou stand'st between a father and a suitor,
> Both striving for an interest in thy heart.
> He courts thee for affection, I for duty;
> He as a servant pleads, but by the privilege
> Of nature though I might command, my care
> Shall only counsel what it shall not force.   (I.ii.93-100)

As old Huntly makes it clear that he gives Katherine her freedom of choice, daughter and suitor alike are touched by his wisdom and goodness. So, too, are we meant to be.

Among the fine Scots, it is Huntly who bears away the bell. This sturdy, crusty old fellow, who swears by St. Andrew in his second speech and again in his fourth, and who speaks more lines in the play than anyone else but Henry and the pretender, is Ford's major means to persuade us of the attractiveness of the Scots. Although he identifies himself modestly as "a plain subject, / Nor more nor less" (II.iii.93-94), he is actually, of course, the Earl of Huntly, leader of the Gordon clan and a splendid ancestor for any Huntly who might be living during the reign of James VI. It may therefore help to recall that the Huntly of James's time was George Gordon, sixth Earl, a royal favorite who was loved by the king both unwisely and too well. Willson describes him: "Young, handsome, gay and attractive, Huntly in 1588 had married Lady Henrietta Stuart, a sister of the young Duke of Lennox, and was thereby admitted to the innermost circle of those on whom the King lavished affection" (pp. 88-89). For the marriage of Huntly at Holyrood, James even bestirred himself to write a masque in which he himself was to appear simultaneously—and extraordinarily—as both player and king. Thereafter, says Willson, Huntly "was almost a member of the royal family...." No matter how extreme his actions—notably his traitorous offer to help Philip of Spain should he decide to send an armada to Scotland—James repeatedly forgave him. The day after the armada incident broke, James was dining with Huntly, "yea, kissing him at times to the amazement of many...."[4] James may have perceived some political advantage in allowing maneuvering room to Huntly and certain other Catholic lords, but his personal partiality toward Huntly was nonetheless unbounded. As far as Ford's play is concerned, then, one should observe that the name of Huntly, which was especially beloved by James VI and I, is given to an unusually well developed character who is a wholly admirable and sympathetic Scot. Though his personality bears no discernible resemblance to that of James's favorite, he is nonetheless the very pattern of a good ancestor.

If, indeed, there is an indirect compliment here, then it fits well with the larger fact that James, almost from the beginning of his English reign, had been concerned that the English and Scots get on well together. As Akrigg has shown, "the flow of letters that passed between London and Edinburgh show how close an eye King James kept on Scottish affairs...."[5] Moreover, "James's continuing supervision of Scottish affairs helped obviate any really major crises until death ended his reign..." (p. 12). Charles was a very different sort of man. As Carlton observes, "of the approximately two thousand letters that were sent to Scotland between 1625 and 1635 in the king's name not a single one was written in his hand."[6] Unlike James, Charles did not understand or really like the Scots.

CHAPTER EIGHT

Favorites and Fools

Ford's treatment of what one might call Henry's support group is also instructive. Here the most striking figure is Daubeney, one of the rare "Minions to noblest fortunes" (III.i.46), according to the king. "*Giles Lord Dawbney*," says Gainsford, was "a man of wisedome, experience and fidelitie" (p. 54); "of great sufficiency and valour," Bacon adds, "the more because he was gentle and moderate" (p. 168). All true, perhaps. And Giles Daubeney had been one of Henry of Richmond's companions in exile in Britanny. Daubeney, in short, served his king both long and well in a variety of capacities, and upon his death he was placed in a fine alabaster tomb in the middle of the Chapel of St. Paul at Westminster, just at the foot of the steps to the chapel which Henry had designed for himself and his own posterity.

The praise for Daubeney that is implicit in Ford's play may have flowed over the brim to be shared with several historical successors who bore the similar name of D'Aubigny. Esmé Stewart, Lord of Aubigny, a French nobleman but of Scotland's royal house (he was a cousin to James's father, Darnley), came to Scotland in 1579. A polished man of the world, this sixth Seigneur d'Aubigny clearly dazzled young James, who was still in his impressionable teens. Whatever the nature of their intimacy (some think it involved a sexual element), Bingham acutely observes that D'Aubigny soon became the family that James lacked, and James at once set about to repay the older man for his own happiness.[1] In 1580, a new and powerful office, that of heritable Great Chamberlain and First Gentleman of the Chamber, was made for him. (In Ford's play, we are present when Henry VII makes Sir Giles Daubeney Chamberlain.) That same year D'Aubigny was created Earl of Lenox (a title James himself had previously held), and in 1581 Lord Aubigny, Earl of Darnley, and Duke of Lenox—thus becoming the only Duke in Scotland. And when Lenox died in 1583, the griefstricken James wrote *Ane Metaphoricall Invention . . . Called Phoenix* (1584).

In the autumn of 1583, meanwhile, James had sent for his favorite's nine-year-old son, Ludovick Stuart, who eventually became a sort of phoenix *redivivus*. What James could no longer give to his beloved first

51

Duke and Great Chamberlain he now gave to the second. In May of 1603, when James moved from Theobalds toward London, it was the younger Lenox who bore the Sword of Honor before the king. His unique position of prominence in Scotland was to continue in England, furthermore, for there also he outranked all the rest of the nobility. Understandable it is, then, when we find the young John Ford in 1606 composing *Honor Trimphant: or The Peeres Challenge* and giving the first position to "the most noble Lord, the Duke of *Lennox*" (A2v), ahead of the Earls of Arundel, Pembroke, and Montgomery. In November of 1616 Ludovick became Lord Steward, the white-staff officer charged with managing the king's own household. Hence Jonson punned in his gypsy masque of 1621, "To prove a false steward you'll find much ado, / Being a true one by blood and by office too" (ll. 622-623). It is striking also to find this treasured royal friend and Spanish pensioner addressed by the Spanish teacher introduced here earlier, Juan de Luna. Luna's dedication to *A Short and Compendious Art* describes Lenox as "vn abismo, herario, y deposito de muchas ciencias, y lenguas (particularmente de la Castellana)" (A3r & v)—all in all, it would appear, an appropriate man for James to put in charge of welcoming the *infanta*. (The latter point should not be pressed hard, though, for Lenox, always a faithful servant to his king, nevertheless had misgivings about the Spanish marriage.) By that time—1623—he had also been created Earl of Newcastle-upon-Tyne and, significantly, Duke of Richmond. When he died of the "spotted ague" in February of 1624, he, too, like Sir Giles Daubeney, was buried in Westminster Abbey, in fact in the splendid chapel of Henry VII, only a few feet from the place where James himself would soon be laid. Later that same year Abraham Darcie hastened to raise in words *A Monumentall Pyramide*, which told how the king's old friend had left "*a deathles memory and fame, / To be an Honor to* Aubigny's *Name*..." (A4r).

Ludovick was succeeded by his younger brother, Esmé. A well-known man and masquer at James's court (Jonson's "lou'd AUBIGNY," Epigram 127), Esmé had become seventh Seigneur d'Aubigny on the death of his father in 1583 and now was Duke of Lenox, but he himself died only a few months after Ludovick, in the summer of 1624. Esmé's successors, in turn, included among others James Stuart, fourth Duke of Lenox and second Duke of Richmond, and Lord George Stuart, ninth Seigneur d'Aubigny, both of whom proved to be devoted royalists, but neither of whom stood to Charles as his predecessors had to James.

It is suggested here, in short, that seventeenth-century auditors heard

Fig. 9.　The white staff of office as shown in a portrait
of Ludovick Stuart, Duke of Lenox and Richmond.

something quite different from what our own contemporaries have heard when Ford has the English king address his right-hand man as "Dear friend, / My faithful Daubeney" (III.i.91-92; cf. also IV.iv.84). Whereas Philip Edwards has found Daubeney "sycophantic," and Gifford thinks him "more forward with his flattery than any of the [other] courtiers,"[2] Daubeney probably is the means by which Ford records some of the things he most wants to say about Henry. In fact, the prominence Ford assigns him is worth questioning. Not only is Daubeney the man who eventually captures Warbeck and brings him back to Henry, thus helping materially to solve Henry's greatest problem in the play (historical fact was helpful, of course), but throughout the play Ford draws attention to Daubeney by giving him more lines than any other spokesman for England save the king himself. At the opening of the play, when Ford has a good deal of exposition to manage and a number of characters to maneuver, he allows Henry (with seventy-one lines) and Daubeney (with thirty-one) to monopolize two-thirds of the scene. In III.i, when Henry appears with gorget and sword but does not fight, Daubeney comes to report on the outcome of the Cornish rebellion, and, except for sixteen lines spoken by others, the king and his friend again share the scene. And in IV.iv Ford not only places Daubeney at the king's side again, but again he has these two speak most of the scene.

One of the play's own commentaries on such prominence may be found in the opening scene's triad of characters, made up of Henry *"supported to his throne by* STANLEY *and* DURHAM," for the rotten supporter must be removed, and a strong, true one placed in its stead. Henry's opening speech, the first in the play, closes with the lines, "And yet for all this glorious work of peace / Ourself is scarce secure" (I.i.13-14). Hence Henry's later lines, succinct but important, "Die all our griefs with Stanley! Take this staff / Of office Daubeney; henceforth be our chamberlain" (II.ii.123-124). By calling for a white staff to be carried onstage—a visible emblem of loyal support and power—Ford dispossesses Stanley, exalts Daubeney, and synchronically reminds those who know already that Daubeney's Jacobean counterpart is one of the king's royal whitestaves. Fig. 9 not only gives us some idea of the splendid appearance of Ludovick Stuart *cum* staff, but also suggests the visual, onstage force of such a property. All the more noteworthy it is, then, that in the final moments of the play, just after Daubeney is allowed to give the best summation of Perkin ("impostor beyond precedent" [V.ii.208]), Henry appears again in the center of a triad, and again with Durham, but this time with Hialas on his other side. Ford now wants to leave us with a living emblem of peaceful unity. In the main, nevertheless, Daubeney is the figure closest to Henry, and therefore remindful of his Jacobean successor, Ludovick, who had been close to James ever since the two were boys, despite the comings and goings of other favorites. During an illness that James underwent in 1619, when it was thought he would die, the three men he commended to Charles as most faithful were Buckingham (the reigning favorite), Digby (England's most skilled diplomat in Anglo-Spanish affairs), and Lenox, his best old friend.

In his *History of Great Britain* (1653) Arthur Wilson relates the king's reaction when his friend unexpectedly predeceased him:

> That morning [12 February 1624] the *Parliament* was to begin, the King missed the *Duke* of *Richmond's* attendance, who being a constant observer of him at all times, the King, as it were, wanted one of his Limbs to support the *Grandure* of *Majesty*, at the first solemn meeting of a *Parliament*, and calling for him with earnestness, a Messenger was dispatched to his Lodgings in Hast.... (p. 257)

When James realized that death had taken from him the support of this justly valued "limb," "he would not adorn himself that day to ride in his *Glories* to the *Parliament*, but put it off to the nineteenth of *February*..." (p. 257).

Although Ford depicts Daubeney as Henry's mainstay, he also gives honorable mention to Oxford and Surrey. Like two bright jewels in the royal crown, these two representatives of the old English nobility help establish Henry's stature and strength, commanding as much interest in the play for what they are as for who they are. At the time she is captured, Katherine makes this point by the cast of a compliment (a striking one, coming from a pretender's wife) offered to Oxford: "Your king is herein royal, / That by a peer so ancient in desert / As well as blood commands us to his presence" (V.i.97-99). Ford gives Surrey but one major scene (IV.i), and yet makes him the worthy receiver of James IV's chivalrous challenge to single combat.

Given the constraints of historical fact, Ford did especially well with the backup teams he managed to place behind each of his three regal figures. With the recognition that each team helps in varied ways to qualify and define the leader it serves, one should glance also at Warbeck's support group. Warbeck's English followers of any worth are taken from him early and never depicted in his presence. With his Scottish support comprised mainly of James IV (who eventually learns

Fig. 10.   Wild Irish as pictured in John Derricke, *The Image of Irelande* (1581).

better) and Katherine (his enforced bride), he is left with a handful of clownish "counsellors" (I.iii.58; II.iii.137) and their crafty French ringleader. At the initial appearance of this group with Perkin in II.i, not one of them speaks. At the outset, then, we learn that they are voiceless, and soon thereafter we learn that their silence is that of the void. In two of their scenes (III.iv and IV.iii) only Frion is assigned lines of his own. In another (V.ii), all appear but only one says more than "Mercy, mercy!" (l. 119). And in V.iii, as in II.i, every one of these comic mannikins is silent. Since we need to hear no more than we do from them to know their quality, any more than we need to eat all an egg to know it rotten, their silence not only speeds the action but also enhances their characterization, and, furthermore, the characterization of all in the play who are thereby made to seem brighter and more articulate.

One can emphasize this point by turning to II.iii, where Frion persuades his companions to perform "some show, some masque, or some device" on behalf of the supposed "Richard." Ever the brains of the group, Frion says, "as for the conceit, / Refer it to my study; the performance / You shall share a thanks in" (ll. 163-165). The facts that Heron has had dancing lessons and Skelton has had experience with both costumes and cross-capers, and perhaps especially that Astley has attended Irish hub-bubs and John-a-Water has been mayor of Cork— all these details should be called to mind when at last we come to the wedding celebration in III.ii. There we find four Scotch antics and four wild Irishmen—at least half of whom we ought to recognize. With their long hair and close-fitting "trowses" (both called for by the stage direction), the dim-brained, uncultivated counsellors are neatly and comically reduced to what, metaphorically, they really are. (Fig. 10 may help to convey an idea of how the "wild Irish" were supposed to look.[3] Furthermore, when we read that "*The Maskers dance*," we have every reason to suspect that what Ford really has set up is an anti-masque. Huntly, who might be supposed to have overheard a rehearsal of the presentation, indulges in some adoxographic praise of their "rare discord of bells, pipes and tabors" (III.ii.4; n.b. the bagpipe in the left foreground of Fig. 10). In fact, he provides what we may take to be a built-in stage direction for the comedians' eventual performance when he speaks of their "Hotch-potch" of noises sounding "like so many quiristers of Bedlam" (ll. 5-6). Since Warbeck's four counsellors are the only performers specified to appear here (Frion's absence is remarked [III.ii.121-123]), we may assume that they and the four (doubtless doubling) "Scottish" players who join them (III.ii.94-95) are in effect inserted into and meant to contrast to a main masque that is comprised of the brilliant but insubstantial self-presentation of Warbeck himself. That Ford might have countenanced such a reading is suggested quite clearly in the opening scene of the play when Henry speaks of Warbeck's "pageant majesty" (I.i.3), and in Warbeck's own first entry, a carefully designed ceremony of wordless salutation that is carried out to the sound of "sprightly music" (II.i.38) and witnessed from above by an onstage audience ("Let us observe 'em and be silent," says Katherine [II.i.17]). If, as seems plausible, Warbeck enters with an attendant bearing the ensign or banner of Richard, Duke of York ("The young duke is at hand," says James IV; "majesty encounters majesty" [ll. 35, 39]), then the pretender is shown to be literally as well as figuratively advancing under false colors. In Act V, furthermore, Ford has Henry bid Warbeck cast off his "antic pageantry, and now appear / In your own nature..." (V.ii.88). Now that Warbeck's actions are played out, Henry would have the young man cast his eyes backward to consider

What revels in combustion through our kingdom
A frenzy of aspiring youth hath danced,
Till, wanting breath, thy feet of pride have slipped
To break thy neck.   (V.ii.50-53)

Meanwhile, if we can agree that it is Warbeck's support-team who kick up their heels in the comic dance—rather like the wild Irishmen in Jonson's *Irish Masque* of 1613 ("Chreesh blesh ty shweet faish, king Yamish" [ll. 21-22])—then we can chalk up yet another scene in which Warbeck's mainstays are wordless. At the same time, they characterize themselves unmistakably—and their rudesby costumes do not hinder the effect—as dancing fools.

Working with history and in many ways keeping close to it, Ford nonetheless is highly creative in presenting contrasted support groups for James, Henry, and Warbeck. All the more remarkable it is, then, that the characters of Huntly and Daubeney, depicted at the courts of James IV and Henry VII, respectively, were succeeded in real life by other men bearing the same names and just happening to be among the greatest favorites of King James VI and I.

CHAPTER NINE

The King and the Pretender

On our way to some conclusions, let us look briefly at Henry and then Warbeck. During this process, Figs. 11 and 12, which reproduce what are probably the best surviving likenesses of the living Henry and Warbeck, may help to keep vivid in our minds not only Ford's dual focus in the play, but also the fact that he is simultaneously creating, shaping, and shading characters and working with certain historical givens.

Since much is made in the play of Warbeck's verbal facility, and especially since his fate takes him into both Scottish and English settings, and since the title of the play bears his name, we might expect the pretender to be the major speaker in the play. Actually, King Henry is. We have seen already how Henry in a formal, regal mode dominates the symmetrical opening and closing moments of the play, the ultimate effect of which framing may be to suggest that the intervening scenes are so much toil and trouble on the way to achieving stability. Moreover, as the play gets underway, it is Henry, not Warbeck, who dominates not only the opening scene, but also the third of the three scenes in Act I (ii. is set in Scotland), whereas Warbeck is not brought onstage until II.i, and then the colorful young pretender must share our attention with the colorful young King James. In other words, though our interest in Warbeck is major, it should not deflect us from recognizing that, insofar as the overall schema of the play is concerned (and this is true, too, of Bacon's *Historie*), the pretender is but a major problem posed for the more central character, the king.

While it may be argued in great detail that Ford is fundamentally concerned with presenting Henry as a good, wise king—and *ipso facto* as a suitably admirable ancestor of James VI and I—readers have occasionally gone off with Gifford to see Ford's Henry as "a most faithful portraiture of the cold, calculating, stern, shrewd, and avaricious Henry" (II, 128). Philip Edwards thinks that Ford makes Henry's regal rights questionable, and then portrays him as a ruthless Machiavel (p. 26). Florence Ali writes of "Henry's serious shortcomings," holding that his "bold exterior conceals an inner nervous timidity"; "his refusal to see Stanley before execution may be attributed ... to weakness"; and "he is 'frighted' with what even he admits are only 'false apparitions / Of pageant Majestie.'"[1] Space does not permit commenting on each of these points, but to cast some light on the path, we should recall that Ford's handling of Henry is notably gentler than that of his major source, which is itself basically laudatory (Bacon holds up Henry, whatever his flaws, as "a wise man, and an excellent King").[2] Even though one may argue that Ford hazards a humanizing foible or two in handling Henry, the basic image he builds is overwhelmingly favorable —as some readers certainly have recognized. H. J. Oliver takes the extreme stand: "Ford is careful to present Henry all the time as the ideal monarch."[3] The most thorough student of the subject, moreover, Donald Anderson, says not only that Ford's Henry is "flawless," but also that the playwright treats him "more favorably than did any of the chroniclers."[4] This point is important, and Anderson's next one more important still: "Sometimes Ford alters history to increase Henry's statecraft."[5] How and why does Ford do this? Should we not take notice when he creates opportunities for character after character to praise Henry? No mere mute witnesses, Daubeney, Oxford, Surrey, Durham, Urswick, and even Lambert Simnel praise him for his mercy, bounty, gentleness, sweetness, wisdom, and so on—which are not all traits credited to the historical Henry VII. Are Henry's hands stained by putting Stanley to death? Durham explains that it was Stanley's own "treasons / Condemned him, sir, which were as clear and manifest / As foul and dangerous" (II.ii.1-3). Henry is absolved. One reason for us to get such matters in focus here is that the monarch's wisdom, his generosity, his striving for peace, and his concern for unifying Scotland and England were all matters of concern to James VI and I.

So also was the royal gift of prophecy. In writing of the union, James had acknowledged "the prophecie to be trew of my wise Grandfather *Henry* the seuenth, who foretold that the lesser Kingdome... would follow the greater..." (*Works*, 329). As for James himself as seer, Arthur M. Clark has pointed out that a reference in *Macbeth* to King Edward's "heavenly gift of prophecy" (IV.iii.157) is probably an allusion to an ability of James that was accepted by the bishops at the Hampton Court Conference of 1604.[6] In Ford the comparable verbal acknowledgment comes when Daubeney says, "Wise Henry / Divines aforehand of events" (IV.iv.66-67). Virtually the next moment, moreover, an apparent illustration is forthcoming when Henry orders his army to Salisbury, where, as Daubeney remarks, "all is peace" (l. 84). Somehow Henry knows that soon there will be a need for royal troops in that region. But Ford's handling of this fact is subtle. On the one hand, as Ure observes, Ford presents the details of the business in such a way that Henry's "foresight ... can hardly be disentangled from the excellence of his intelligence-service" (p. 109). On the other hand, Ford has the king himself specifically distinguish himself from his noble followers by remarking, "You're men know how to do, not to forethink" (l. 88). In either case, of course, this is a king who knows what he is doing.

Although Ford's play is concerned with various threats to Henry's kingship, the character who has commanded most interest is the apparently noble Warbeck. We may find ourselves asking, therefore, as

Fig. 11. A polychrome bust of Henry VII, ca. 1508-1509.

61

Fig. 12.   Perkin Warbeck as depicted in a sketch from the
Town Library of Arras.

Cervantes asks in *Don Quixote*, at what point does acting like a great man make one great? For of course there are clues aplenty that Ford's Warbeck is *acting* like a great man. The play in which he appears is called *Perkin Warbeck*, which is not likely, after all, to lead any playgoer or playreader to anticipate seeing *The Tragedy of Richard, Duke of York.* The real tragedy for James VI and I would have been that any such prince had survived. Within the play, furthermore, as anyone who holds the script in hand may see, all of the pretender's lines are assigned to a character named Perkin Warbeck. Time and again we are reminded that it is someone called Warbeck who speaks. No lines are labeled with the name of "Richard." And lest the haze of time becloud the onomastic clarity of the impostor's name, we may turn to John Speed, who explains in his *History of Great Britaine* (1611) that "The English in contempt (and for a note perhaps of his forraine birth) did afterward call him by a diminutiue of his name, *Peterkin* or *Perkin*" (p. 737). For corroboration we may turn directly to Gainsford or Bacon, where we find that "Perkin" is a form suggesting cowardliness, effeminateness, and childishness. Even if such meanings strike us as extreme or beside the point (though both of Ford's sources did include them, and though Ford has Crawford refer to Warbeck as "Effeminately dolent" [III.iv.76]), it is worth bearing in mind that the play, in effect, is called *Little Peter Warbeck.*

At the same time, Ford immensely enhances Warbeck's dignity and stature by making him a believer in his own grand claims. Almost at the beginning of Ford scholarship, Gifford observed that "Perkin has no soliloquies, no side speeches, to compromise his public assertions; and it is pleasing to see with what ingenuity Ford has preserved him from the contamination of real history, and contrived to sustain his dignity to the last with all imaginable decorum..." (II, 127). Even alone with Frion, his campaign manager, Warbeck passionately maintains that he really is Richard (IV.ii.8-12). Understandably, then, Warbeck has evoked a wide range of reactions from scholars. Some hold that he is insane, some that he is deluded.[7] Some hold that he is the means which enables Ford "to distinguish between two kinds of reality—one external, historical, and political, the other internal, ethical, and psychological"; or an illustration of how man may transcend mortality and change through art, or even of the recently fashionable "self-fashioning Renaissance spirit in action, striving both to refine and to define itself."[8]

While we are weighing such readings, though, we should bear in mind that if Warbeck were made to seem any less noble, attractive, and

63

generally wonderful, there would follow at least two major consequences, neither good for Ford's play. First, the Scottish king's acceptance of Warbeck, which is necessitated by historical fact, would have made James IV seem either a good deal more gullible or a good deal more Machiavellian. Neither is desirable, since the race of Jameses still occupies the throne. Second, Ford would have gained little by pitting his idealized English monarch against a nonentity. If a Warbeck play is to work at all, Warbeck must have some attractive features. We should not overlook Anderson's crucial observation that whereas "Ford presents Warbeck sympathetically,... Bacon, Gainsford, and the other chroniclers did just the opposite."[9] Since it is Henry whom Ford has chosen to depict as most wise, just, and good, it would be a bit trying to watch this English king and his nobles rallying boldly to squash a "glowworm" (IV.iv.34) who lacks glimmer. In Shakespeare's *1 Henry IV*, similarly, Hal would come off far less well were he not given a young opponent who, though flawed, is worthy. Furthermore, it is the nature of a pretender play to exploit the question of the pretender's identity. Jonas Barish goes so far as to say that "Ford... invites us throughout, and more strongly as the play nears its end, to entertain the hypothesis that Perkin may be telling the truth."[10] But even if we see here some tempting territory for our colleagues the deconstructionists, we are never in much doubt that the hypothesis is wrong. As Ford observes in his Prologue, the whole business is not merely "known" but "famous" (ll. 15, 16). In fact, the opening scene—where a barrage of epithets is fired at the absent Warbeck—closes with what may be not merely a commonplace, but also an evocative reminiscence of the famous and reassuring ploy that Shakespeare allows himself and Prince Hal at the end of I.ii in *1 Henry IV*. In Ford's version, Henry forecasts, "these clouds will vanish, / The sun will shine at full..." (I.i.140-141). Fascinating in himself, Warbeck is also fundamentally useful to Ford for providing a foil that brings out King Henry's genuinely regal qualities.

Aside from the pretender's rhetorical skill (wasted and abused because put to an unworthy end) and his idealism (undercut because erected on lies), one of his characteristics most likely to have resonated in the reign of James VI and I is what we might call his supernatural tonality. From the time we first hear about him until the play concludes, we are given to think that there is something special about Warbeck. An air of mystery serves to make his capabilities appear greater than they are, and also to help explain his influence over others. Its underlying nature as suggested by Ford invites particular interest, moreover, by being a matter known to interest King James. The first line of the play describes Henry as "haunted," and the second one refers to Warbeck as a false apparition. In the second speech the clergyman Durham explains that "The rage of malice / Conjures fresh spirits with the spells of York . . ." (I.i.14-15). As Daubeney and Oxford describe matters, Warbeck's presence in the land may be ascribed not merely to the machinations of Margaret of Burgundy, sister of Edward IV, but to "the unbottomed mine / Of devilish policies" to which she has access (I.i.42-62). Up in Scotland, Crawford thinks witchcraft must be involved when Warbeck appears to charm James IV out of his common sense (II.iii.5-6). Even Henry refers to "The witch-craft wherewith young king James is bound" (III.i.34). And Urswick, too, speaks of Warbeck's witchcraft (V.iii.15, 104-110). Such passages help not only to exculpate those who are taken in by Warbeck, but also to darken his origins, especially his period of Burgundian training. They also remind us that James VI and I, author of *Daemonologie* (1597), with its section on the *"kindes of Spirites that troubles men or women,"* took especial pride in exposing witch-impostors.

EPILOGUE

Nowadays it appears that no truly definitive interpretation of this or any other play will ever be possible, especially if one has to consider the variables involved in actual playhouse productions. Before we sink into the black holes of our own computers, however, we should keep looking for life-lines, not excluding those thrown out by authors. As the present essay began with a cluster of such clues tossed out by Ford, it now closes with three more. Each of them—and others could be cited—exemplifies Ford's tendency in *Perkin Warbeck* to thrust against and sometimes beyond his self-imposed historical boundaries.

First detail: when Richard Fox, Bishop of Durham, pleases his royal master mightily, Ford has Henry exclaim, "My bishop is a jewel tried and perfect; / A jewel, lords" (IV.iv.89-90). Henry's praise is acceptable either at the most superficial metaphorical level or at a more complex level involving jewels as traditional emblems of virtue, but its built-in repetition may also wittily invite us to compare—if only fleetingly— Bishop Richard Fox with Bishop John Jewel (1522-1571), one of the most famous clerics of his day, a native of Ford's own Devonshire, and one who was still very much alive in his many writings. Jewel's landmark *Apologia ecclesiae anglicanae*, which had first appeared in 1562, was printed again in the early part of the reigns of both James (1606) and Charles (1626), and many other times as well, and a folio collection of his *Works* made its initial appearance in James's time (1609; 1611 *bis*). Because Jewel had come to be regarded over the years as one of the most articulate and important champions of the church of which James was head, perhaps we may be justified in asking if his suggestive name might not have been useful for casting warm rays of light on the admirable bishop in Ford's play.

Second detail: when the traitor Sir William Stanley delivers his final speech with an ax-carrying executioner waiting at his side, he asks

> To be remembered to my noble brother,
> Derby, my much grieved brother. O, persuade him
> That I shall stand no blemish to his house
> In chronicles writ in another age. (II.ii.99-102)

Since the first Earl of Derby, Thomas Stanley (earldom: 1485-1504), was the husband of Henry VII's mother (Margaret Beaufort was Countess of Richmond and Derby), it was clearly advisable to clear him

66

for the sake of both Henry VII *and* James VI and I. Furthermore, in Ford's own present chronicle, which is surely "writ in another age," there is nothing to be gained by sullying the name of the then-current William Stanley, sixth Earl of Derby (earldom: 1594-1642). Earl William was not only a distant relation of James VI and I, but also a man with a particular passion for the stage, himself a playwright and composer who had variously known the great gratification of watching his wife Elizabeth (daughter of the seventeenth Earl of Oxford) and his son James (named after the king) and his daughter-in-law Charlotte participating in masques at court.[1]

And third: in his Epilogue, where he is no longer writing speeches for particular characters, Ford quite naturally relates his play to times subsequent to those he has depicted. More particularly, he hopes his play will succeed in picturing "What can to theatres of greatness fall" (l. 4). That is, having made use of theatrical imagery within the play itself, he now presumes that what transpires in a literal theater has the capability of showing an audience what can happen in figurative "theatres of greatness." King James himself, certainly, was familiar with the ubiquitous metaphor of the king and the player. Even if we did not know about the lines he penned for his own lips to speak in the wedding masque for Huntly and his bride back in 1588, we still would have his on-target observation in *Basilikon Doron*: "It is a trew old saying, That a King is as one set on a stage..." (*Works*, 43). Now Ford says here that players in a place devoted to playing can clarify figuratively (in this case by enacting a well-known story from history) the kinds of playing that occur in the highest places in the land. Ford's tenses in the passage are worth watching: "Here has appeared," he writes, "what can... fall" (ll. 1, 4). The action is over, but its implications linger. Like most rhetorical constructs, the play is future-directed, and to give life to the perception that what one sees here is of more than fleeting importance, Ford has meticulously explored and continuously suggested the similarities of the past to his own present.

This study of Ford's *Perkin Warbeck* has been premised on the perception that history takes on some of the coloration of the present in which it is recollected. It has been premised also on the corollary perception that a literary work which attempts to represent some past time is going to represent its own as well. In historical drama, topicality of some sort is virtually inevitable, and indeed the more so if, as in the Renaissance, writers and readers are in the habit of consciously seeking parallels between past and present. One of the basic questions appropriate to

67

historiography is therefore appropriate in a study of *Perkin Warbeck*: why was this particular subject investigated at that particular time? And in the case of *Perkin Warbeck* this question points up the need to answer also the question, what *was* its particular time?

One can make significant inroads into these matters by noting the books by Gainsford (1618) and Bacon (1622), and one should bear in mind that Warbeck had already been represented onstage before Gainsford wrote. But perhaps most important of all in looking for the time, one should recall the profound reassurance and pleasure that King James appears to have taken from the paralleling of Henry VII with himself. Moreover, as Goldberg rightly recalls, Spenser's unfavorable representation of Mary Queen of Scots had much earlier and quite explicitly drawn forth an expression of James's belief in the powers of literary representation.[2] If literature did not have such powers, in fact, no king or committee would try to control it. With this observation we may couple Norbrook's that "even before he came to England he had started to use the drama to reinforce his cult of kingship."[3] Through the years, furthermore, various sorts of English dramatic writings continued to demonstrate an alert responsiveness to James's interests.[4] In Ford, then, we should not fail to note that the representation of James's crucial ancestor is resoundingly favorable. That the character of the challenging pretender is simultaneously depicted favorably is at least partly clarified when we see that the dramatist thereby enhances the quality of both the charming, impetuous, Scottish king and also the English king who must bring the impostor to heel. Nor should we chairbound readers of the text fail to remark the semiotic, theatrical force of the fact that Warbeck enacts most of his long final scene while padlocked in "his majesty's new stocks" (V.iii.2; their very newness may imply Henry's habitual clemency). It is here that Warbeck's counsellors are shown with him one last time, totally silent now and each wearing about the neck a halter that emblematically conveys despair and literally marks attendance on Warbeck in death (V.iii.185-186). Even in his last moments, as he stands near the brink, moreover, Warbeck still prophesies that he and his counsellors will be styled "Kings o'er Death" (l. 207). Throughout the play and even at its end, then, Ford is exploring the quality of power. Challenging as the paradoxes relating to Warbeck may be to our thoughts and imaginations, however, this story of an impostor is finally but one intriguing element—granted, a major one—in the subsuming business of Henry's stabilization of his kingdom.

To suggest here a new "present" for *Perkin Warbeck* is not merely to suggest changing a couple of digits in the annals of English drama, but also to encourage a fresh look at the complex materials which comprise Ford's play, and particularly to call attention to some unifying qualities in it which we have tended to overlook. It is by no means to deny the intriguing, multiple perspectives of the play, the hall-of-mirrors quality discerned by us all, but to point out that Ford raises his questions about this "famous" action in terms of a carefully circumscribed area of historicity and conservative praise. To miss this is to depoliticize and therefore, to a large extent, to enervate the play. Whatever one thinks of conservatism, then or now, it is hard to imagine a story from earlier English history that could have been more suitable for playing on the stage in the early 1620s, and it is hard to imagine a play being crafted in this period so as to bring out more issues bearing on both of its times. King James of Great Britain, proud descendant of Tudor and Stuart, Lancaster and York, the uniter of the crowns of England and Scotland who was convinced that the genuine peace-maker is blessed, was during this period making preparations for yet another Prince of Wales to wed yet another Spanish *infanta*. The tableau at the end of the play, presenting Henry VII at the physical center between Durham and Hialas ("two / ... ministers ... of blessed fate" [IV.iii.31-32]), suggests fresh hopes for England and Spain alike, but above all, and by means of a sort of ceremonial shorthand, it figures forth national and international unity and peace. Because of King Henry's wisdom, the throne has been shored up and made firm. All of this would have helped to reassure not only King James VI and I, but also all of the English who were either pro-Spanish or simply hopeful for good things to come from a Spanish alliance. In the years after 1623, probably even during the last quarter of 1623, much of the matter of the play would have seemed passé to some and irritating or worse to others, but wherever one stood politically, in 1622 and most of 1623 it is likely to have appeared broadly traditionalist and supportive, grateful and gratulatory for what had been achieved, and a presage, for good or ill, of what was to come.

NOTES

NOTES TO PROLOGUE

1 *The Jacobean and Caroline Stage*, III (Oxford, 1956; 1967 printing), 455.
2 *A Critical Edition of Ford's Perkin Warbeck* (Seattle), pp. 31-35.
3 Leech, *John Ford and the Drama of His Time* (London, 1957), and Ribner, *The English History Play in the Age of Shakespeare* (London, 1965; 1st ed., Princeton, 1957).
4 Edwards, "The Royal Pretender in Massinger and Ford," *Essays and Studies*, 27 (1974), 35; Wikander, "Strange Truths: English Historical Drama in the Seventeenth Century," *Genre*, 9 (1976), 203; and Farr, *John Ford and the Caroline Theatre* (New York, 1979), 123. Anyone interested in pursuing this matter and others relating to Ford will be aided by Kenneth Tucker, *A Bibliography of Writings by and about John Ford and Cyril Tourneur* (Boston, 1977); Terence P. Logan and Denzell S. Smith, ed. *The Later Jacobean and Caroline Dramatists: A Survey and Bibliography of Recent Studies in English Renaissance Drama* (Lincoln, Neb., 1978); and Rachel Fordyce, *Caroline Drama: A Bibliographic History of Criticism* (Boston, 1978).
5 Ure, ed. *The Chronicle History of Perkin Warbeck* (Manchester, 1968), p. xxx. All citations from the play will be drawn from this edition.
6 *John Ford*, TEAS 129 (New York, 1972), pp. 80-81.
7 Henry Weber, ed. *The Dramatic Works of John Ford*, II (Edinburgh, 1811), 4.
8 Harbage, "The Mystery of *Perkin Warbeck*," *Studies in the English Renaissance Drama*, ed. Josephine W. Bennett, Oscar Cargill, and Vernon Hall, Jr. (New York, 1959), pp. 125-141; and Homan, "Dekker as Collaborator in Ford's *Perkin Warbeck*," *ELN*, 3 (1965), 104-106.
9 Ure, ed. *Perkin Warbeck*, pp. xxx-xxxv.
10 Cf. *Macbeth* IV.i, with its show of eight kings. A very different view of Dalyell's speech is given by Ure, "A Pointer to the Date of Ford's 'Perkin Warbeck,'" *NQ*, n.s. 17 (1970), 215-217.

NOTES TO CHAPTER ONE:
A HISTORY COUCHED IN A PLAY

1 *John Ford* (Oxford, 1935), p. 69.
2 "The Tragedies of John Ford," in *The Fine Art of Reading and Other Literary Studies* (London, 1957), p. 86.
3 "*Perkin Warbeck*: A Seventeenth-Century Psychological Play," *SEL*, 4 (1964), 217.
4 Ure ed., pp. 9-10.
5 Ribner, p. 24. More recent and also helpful is Herbert Lindenberger, *Historical Drama: The Relation of Literature and Reality* (Chicago, 1975).

⁶ *Basilikon Doron* (1599), reprinted in *The Political Works of James I*, ed. Charles Howard McIlwain (Cambridge, Mass., 1918), p. 40. Unless otherwise specified, further citations of James's writing are from this edition and designated *Works*.

⁷ *History*, ed. F. J. Levy (Indianapolis, 1972), p. 197; subsequent citations are also from this edition. Bacon, in turn, was availing himself of ready-made imagery: John Speed, in *The History of Great Britaine* (1611), had written of Warbeck as *"an imaginary and Stage-play Prince"* (p. 743), citing Camden as his source.

⁸ *The True Exemplary, and Remarkable History of the Earle of Tirone* (1619), p. 4.

⁹ Anne Barton describes the status of history plays in the earlier seventeenth century in "He That Plays the King: Ford's *Perkin Warbeck* and the Stuart History Play," in Marie Axton and Raymond Williams, ed., *English Drama: Forms and Development* (Cambridge, 1977), pp. 69-93.

NOTES TO CHAPTER TWO:
A SHOW OF KINGS

¹ From "The Beginning of the History of Great Britain," in *History*, ed. Levy, p. 281.

² See also David M. Bergeron, *English Civic Pageantry 1558-1642* (Columbia, S.C., 1971), pp. 77-78; and Graham Parry, *The Golden Age Restor'd: The Culture of the Stuart Court* (New York, 1981), p. 9.

³ *The Letters and the Life of Francis Bacon*, ed. James Spedding, VII (London, 1874), 303.

⁴ William Cobbett, *Cobbett's Parliamentary History of England*, vol. I (London, 1806), col. 1151. Having gone into the subject at great length in order to illuminate *Macbeth*, Henry N. Paul concluded that "James was a genealogist. Only one who keeps in mind the passionate interest which this learned king had in his royal ancestry...can understand certain parts of the play" (*The Royal Play of Macbeth* [New York, 1950], p. 152). For all the contemporary data one could hope to find in a single source, see George Owen Harry, *The Genealogy of the High and Mighty Monarch, James* (1604).

⁵ *Historical Memorials of Westminster Abbey* (London, 1911; 1st ed., 1867; 5th ed., 1882, introduced Stanley's final emendations), p. 525.

NOTES TO CHAPTER THREE:
THREE ROYAL MATCHES

¹ *The Union of the Two Noble and Illustre Famelies of Lancastre & Yorke* (1548), aaa.iiir. For some helpful remarks on Henry's management of events during this crucial early period see S. B. Chrimes, *Henry VII* (Berkeley, California, 1972), esp, pp. 65-67.

[1] Quoted by D. H. Willson, *King James VI and I* (London, 1956), p. 13.

[2] John Nichols, *The Progresses, Processions, and Magnificent Festivities of King James the First*, IV (London, 1828), 1043-44; and Stanley, p. 522.

[3] See also Per Palme, *Triumph of Peace: A Study of the Whitehall Banqueting House* (London, 1957), pp. 233-240; and D. J. Gordon, "Rubens and the Whitehall Ceiling," *The Renaissance Imagination*, ed. Stephen Orgel (Berkeley, 1980), pp. 38-41. There is more than a hint here of James as Solomon, decreeing in this instance that the child be shared, not split. See Julius S. Held, *The Oil Sketches of Peter Paul Rubens: A Critical Catalogue*, I (Princeton, 1980), 204-210.

[4] *Masque of Blackness*, 1. 221, in *Ben Jonson: The Complete Masques*, ed. Stephen Orgel (New Haven, 1969), pp. 55, 56. Subsequent quotations from the maques are from this volume.

[5] Cobbett, cols. 1074-75.

[6] *Tom Tell Troath* (n.d.; STC 23868), p. 2.

[1] *Renaissance Diplomacy* (Baltimore, 1964; c. 1955), p. 231. A great deal of relevant material on this subject has been garnered and placed in perspective by Margot Heinemann in Chapter 10 of her *Puritanism and Theatre: Thomas Middleton and Opposition Drama under the Early Stuarts* (Cambridge, 1980).

[2] Noted by Charles H. Carter, "Gondomar: Ambassador to James I," *Historical Journal*, 7 (1964), 193. Carter sees much more give-and-take than is usually perceived in the James-Gondomar relationship.

[3] A case for the latter point is made in the present writer's "Some New Perspectives on the Spanish Setting of *The Changeling* and Its Source," forthcoming in *Medieval & Renaissance Drama in England*. See Floriana T. Hogan, "Elizabethan and Jacobean Dramas and Their Spanish Sources," in David M. Bergeron, ed. *Research Opportunities in Renaissance Drama*, 19 (Lawrence, Kansas, 1977), 37-47.

[4] See Charles C. Mish, comp., *English Prose Fiction, 1600-1700: A Chronological Checklist* (Charlottesville, Virginia, 1967), pp. 14-15; discussed in my *Golden Tapestry: A Critical Survey of Non-chivalric Spanish Fiction in English Translation (1543-1657)* (Durham, N.C., 1963), p. 221 and *passim*.

[5] Quoted by Nichols, IV, 812.

[6] *Thomas Middleton*, TEAS 139 (New York, 1972), p. 96.

[7] *Considerations upon the Treaty of Marriage Between England and Spain* (1623?), p. 1.

[8] Godfrey Goodman, *The Court of King James the First*, ed. John S. Brewer, I (London, 1839), 362.

[9] Cited by Samuel R. Gardiner, *History of England*, III (London, new impression 1901), 283.

[10] Cobbett, cols. 1326-27.

[11] Gardiner, IV (London, new impression 1901), 190.

[12] John Chamberlain, *The Chamberlain Letters: A Selection*, ed. Elizabeth McClure Thomson (New York, 1965), p. 259.

[13] Quoted by Gardiner, IV, 354.

[14] This and the following cluster of details are gathered from Nichols, IV: 829, 846, 855, 873. Perhaps it should be noted that views on the relative warmth of Charles's welcome vary considerably.

[15] Goodman, II (1839), 295.

[16] To Ford's depiction of Hialas we may contrast his widely scattered but largely negative remarks on Spaniards elsewhere. The most extended occurs in *Love's Sacrifice*, where Fernando warns a traveler that

> In Spain you lose experience; 'tis a climate
> Too hot to nourish arts; the nation proud,
> And in their pride unsociable; the court
> More pliable to glorify itself
> Than do a stranger grace....

(I.i: cited from *John Ford*, ed. Havelock Ellis [New York, 1965 printing], p. 262.) The French here fare better than the Spanish.

[17] Thinking of similar formal scenes in earlier history plays, Martha Hester Fleischer writes thus:

> The tableau effect was... evoked by the symmetrical blocking employed for the group scenes so prevalent in these plays. Or presumably employed, and on cogent grounds. There was not much time for rehearsal, and it is fair to assume that symmetry, "the simplest order in art," recommended itself as the simplest arrangement for blocking. Social decorum suggested ready-made symmetrical arrangements. ... Moreover, "symmetry of proportion, whereby art partakes of reason," was considered the basic principle of beauty by nearly everyone....

(*The Iconography of the English History Play* [Salzburg, 1974], p. 39.) Still more helpful, perhaps, is a comment made by David Bevington in a chapter called "The Language of Ceremony"; writing of Shakespeare, Bevington throws a sidelight on Ford: "These images of order derive their intensity of meaning from the conflict out of which they have grown" (*Action Is Eloquence: Shakespeare's Language of Gesture* [Cambridge, Mass., 1984], p. 139).

Outside *Perkin Warbeck* itself, Ford's own use of a triadic picture—at once formal and packed with implications—is most effective in *The Broken Heart*, where the text calls for three chairs, the middle one for the veiled corpse of Penthea, the other two for Orgilus and Ithocles. Orgilus bids Ithocles, "Take that chair. / I'll seat me here in this. Between us sits / The object of our sorrows" (IV.iv.16-18).

NOTES TO CHAPTER SIX:
TRIUMPHS OF PEACE

1 *The True and Wonderfull History of Perkin Warbeck* (1618), p. 89.
2 Nichols, IV, 625.
3 *A Memorial of All the English Monarchs* (1622), F5v.
4 Cobbett, cols. 1388-89.
5 "Kingship in Ford's *Perkin Warbeck*," *ELH*, 27 (1960), 192.
6 Cited by Charles Carlton, *Charles I* (London, 1983), p. 80.
7 Raymond A. Anselment, "Clarendon and the Caroline Myth of Peace," *Journal of British Studies*, 23 (1984), 37-54.
8 See the discussion of both by Annabel Patterson (in part citing Stephen Orgel) in *Censorship and Interpretation: The Conditions of Writing and Reading in Early Modern England* (Madison, Wisconsin, 1984), pp. 108-111.

NOTES TO CHAPTER SEVEN:
HONORABLE SCOTS

1 Francis Osborne, *Some Traditionall Memorialls* (1658), in *Secret History of the Court of James the First*, I (1811), 254.
2 *The Dramatic Works of John Ford*, II (London, 1827), 94.
3 "The Dramatic Functions of Love in the Tragedies of John Ford," *SP*, 70 (1973), 65.
4 Willson, p. 101, quoting an unnamed contemporary source.
5 Akrigg, ed. *Letters of King James VI & I* (Berkeley, 1984), p. 11.
6 Carlton, pp. 158-159. In contrast, James's achievement has been weighed and praised by Maurice Lee, Jr., in *Government by Pen: Scotland under James VI and I* (Urbana, Ill., 1980); and David Mathew, *Scotland under Charles I* (London, 1955).

NOTES TO CHAPTER EIGHT:
FAVORITES AND FOOLS

1 *The Making of a King: The Early Years of James VI and I* (Garden City, New York, 1969), pp. 152, 131.
2 Edwards, p. 25; Gifford, II, 74.
3 The drawing is reproduced from John Derricke, *The Image of Irelande, with a Discoverie of... Wilde Irish Woodkarne* (1581), reprinted in *A Collection of Scarce and Valuable Tracts* (The Somers Tracts), rev. and aug. Walter Scott, I (London, 1809; 2d ed.), 592. A dangerous, devilish lot, the wild Irish are said to "passe not for civilitie, / nor care for wisdomes lore..." (p. 581). In another connection, Bacon in his *Historie* has occasion to tell how "the wild Irish... fled into the woods and bogs, after their manner" (p. 169). Barnabe Rich, in a chapter called "*From whence it proceedeth, that the* Irish *are so repugnant to the* English," observes that they are not only rude, unclean, and uncivil, but also "apt and ready to commit any kind of mischiefe" (*A New Description of Ireland* [1610], p. 15).

1 *Opposing Absolutes: Conviction and Convention in John Ford's Plays* (Salzburg, 1974), p. 66.

2 P. 65. But see Thomas Wheeler, "The Purpose of Bacon's *History of Henry the Seventh*," *SP*, 54 (1957), 1-13.

3 *The Problem of John Ford* (Carlton, Australia, 1955), p. 104.

4 Ed., *Perkin Warbeck*, p. xv.

5 P. xvi. See also Anderson's *John Ford*, p. 88.

6 *Murder under Trust or The Topical Macbeth* (Edinburgh, 1981), p. 23.

7 E.g., Lawrence Babb, "Abnormal Psychology in John Ford's *Perkin Warbeck*," *MLN*, 51 (1936), 234-237; and Mark Stavig, *John Ford and the Traditional Moral Order* (Madison, 1968), pp. 180, 182-183. One might add that Ford's skill should fascinate a yet wider range of critics than have thus far noticed, for there are enough complicating details here to warrant suggesting that Ford himself initiates a deconstructive process.

8 Tucker Orbison, *The Tragic Vision of John Ford* (Salzburg, 1974), p. 152; Michael Neill, "'Anticke Pageantrie': The Mannerist Art of *Perkin Warbeck*," *RD*, 7 (1976), 117-150; and Joseph Candido, "The 'Strange Truth' of *Perkin Warbeck*," *PQ*, 59 (1980), 300-316. Though the play lies outside her area of interest, Judith H. Anderson suggests that *Perkin Warbeck* may be approached in terms of Donne's "Canonization": sonnets vs. chronicles (*Biographical Truth: The Representation of Historical Persons in Tudor-Stuart Writing* [New Haven, 1984], p. 154).

9 Ed., *Perkin Warbeck*, p. xiv.

10 "*Perkin Warbeck* as Anti-History," *Essays in Criticism*, 20 (1970), 157.

NOTES TO EPILOGUE

1 J. J. Bagley, *The Earls of Derby 1485-1985* (London, 1985), pp. 76-77. Of course Stanley's final words in the play are non-terminous in a yet broader sense: to the extent that the story told here appears in current "chronicles" (such as the present study, it might be argued), they look forward to and beyond the current and eighteenth Earl of Derby, Edward John Stanley, (earldom: 1948-).

2 Jonathan Goldberg, *James I and the Politics of Literature* (Baltimore, 1983), p. xii.

3 David Norbrook, *Poetry and Politics in the English Renaissance* (London, 1984), p. 177. An invaluable predecessor of this work is David Bevington's *Tudor Drama and Politics: A Critical Approach to Topical Meaning* (Cambridge, Mass., 1968).

4 For an extended investigation of such responsiveness in one particular masque, where it is blended with criticism, see the present writer's *Jonson's Gypsies Unmasked: Background and Theme of "The Gypsies Metamorphos'd"* (Durham, N.C., 1975).

WORKS CITED

(N.b. Unless otherwise indicated, the place of publication is London.)

Alemán, Mateo, *The Rogue: Or the Life of Guzman de Alfarache*, trans. James Mabbe (1622); Part Two (1623).

Ali, Florence, *Opposing Absolutes: Conviction and Convention in John Ford's Plays*, Salzburg Studies in English Literature: Jacobean Drama Studies No. 44 (Salzburg, 1974).

Anderson, Donald K., Jr., *John Ford*, TEAS 129 (New York, 1972).

———, "Kingship in Ford's *Perkin Warbeck*," *ELH*, 27 (1960), 177-193.

———, See also *Ford*.

Anderson, Judith H., *Biographical Truth: The Representation of Historical Persons in Tudor-Stuart Writings* (New Haven, 1984).

Anselment, Raymond A., "Clarendon and the Caroline Myth of Peace," *Journal of British Studies*, 23 (Spring, 1984), 37-54.

Babb, Lawrence, "Abnormal Psychology in John Ford's *Perkin Warbeck*," *MLN*, 51 (1936), 234-237.

Bacon, Francis, *The Historie of the Raigne of King Henry the Seventh* (1622).

———, *The History of the Reign of King Henry the Seventh*, ed. F. J. Levy (Indianapolis, 1972).

———, *The Letters and the Life of Francis Bacon*, ed. James Spedding, VII (1874).

Bagley, John J., *The Earls of Derby, 1485-1985* (1985).

Barish, Jonas A., "*Perkin Warbeck* as Anti-History," *Essays in Criticism*, 20 (1970), 151-171.

Barton, Anne, "He That Plays the King: Ford's *Perkin Warbeck* and the Stuart History Play," in Marie Axton and Raymond Williams, ed., *English Drama: Forms and Development* (Cambridge, 1977), pp. 69-93.

Bentley, Gerald E., *The Jacobean and Caroline Stage*, III (Oxford, 1956; 1967 printing).

Bergeron, David M., *English Civic Pageantry 1558-1642* (Columbia, S.C., 1971).

Bevington, David M., *Action Is Eloquence: Shakespeare's Language of Gesture* (Cambridge, Mass., 1984).

———, *Tudor Drama and Politics: A Critical Approach to Topical Meaning* (Cambridge, Mass., 1968).

Bingham, Caroline, *The Making of a King: The Early Years of James VI and I* (Garden City, N.Y., 1969).

Brittin, Norman A., *Thomas Middleton*, TEAS 139 (New York, 1972).

Brooke, Christopher, *The Ghost of Richard the Third*, introd. J. Payne Collier (1884), publication No. 22, vol. 10, of Shakespeare Society of London (Kraus Reprint Ltd., Nendeln, Liechtenstein, 1966).

Candido, Joseph, "The 'Strange Truth' of *Perkin Warbeck*," *PQ*, 59 (1980), 300-316.

Carlton, Charles, *Charles I* (1983).

Carter, Charles H., "Gondomar: Ambassador to James I," *Historical Journal*, 7 (1964), 189-208.

Cecil, David, "The Tragedies of John Ford," in *The Fine Art of Reading and Other Literary Studies* (1957), pp. 79-92.

Cervantes Saavedra, Miguel de, *The Historie of the Valorous and Wittie Knight-errant, Don-Quixote*, trans. Thomas Shelton, I (1612); I and II (1620).

Céspedes y Meneses, Gonzalo de, *Gerardo the Unfortunate Spaniard*, trans. Leonard Digges (1622).

Chamberlain, John, *The Chamberlain Letters: A Selection*, ed. Elizabeth McClure Thomson (New York, 1965).

Chrimes, S. B., *Henry VII* (Berkeley, California, 1972).

Clark, Arthur Melville, *Murder under Trust or The Topical Macbeth* (Edinburgh, 1981).

Cobbett, William, *Cobbett's Parliamentary History of England*, I (1806).

Considerations upon the Treaty of Marriage between England and Spain (1623?).

Cornwallis, William, *The Miraculous and Happie Union of England and Scotland* (1604).

Daniel, Samuel, *A Panegyrike Congratulatory* (1603).

Darcie, Abraham, *A Monumentall Pyramide* (1624).

Derricke, John, *The Image of Irelande, with a Discoverie of . . . Wilde Irish Woodkarne* (1581), reprinted in *A Collection of Scarce and Valuable Tracts*, vol. I (The Somers Tracts), rev. and aug. Walter Scott (1809; 2d ed.).

DuVal, Michael, *The Spanish-English Rose or The English-Spanish Pomgranet* (1623?; ent. to W. Fisher 23 July 1622).

Edwards, Philip, "The Royal Pretender in Massinger and Ford," *Essays and Studies*, 27 (1974), 18-36.

Farr, Dorothy, *John Ford and the Caroline Theatre* (New York, 1979).

Fleischer, Martha Hester, *The Iconography of the English History Play*, Salzburg Studies in English Literature: Elizabethan and Renaissance Studies No. 10 (Salzburg, 1974).

Ford, John, *The Broken Heart*, ed. T. J. B. Spencer (Manchester, 1980).

———, *The Chronicle Historie of Perkin Warbeck* (1634).

———, *The Chronicle History of Perkin Warbeck*, ed. Peter Ure (Manchester, 1968).

———, *A Critical Edition of Ford's Perkin Warbeck*, ed. Mildred Clara Struble (Seattle, 1926).

———, *The Dramatic Works of John Ford*, ed. William Gifford, 2 vols. (1827).

———, *The Dramatic Works of John Ford*, ed. Henry Weber, 2 vols. (Edinburgh, 1811).

———, *Fames Memoriall, or The Earle of Devonshire Deceased* (1606).

———, *Honor Triumphant. Or the Peeres Challenge* (1606).

———, *A Line of Life: Pointing at the Immortalitie of a Vertuous Name* (1620).

————, *Love's Sacrifice*, in *John Ford*, ed. Havelock Ellis (New York, 1965 printing).

————, *Perkin Warbeck*, ed. Donald K. Anderson, Jr. (Lincoln, Neb., 1965).

————, with Thomas Dekker and William Rowley, *The Witch of Edmonton*, ed. Simon Trussler and Jacqui Russell (1983).

Fordyce, Rachel, *Caroline Drama: A Bibliographic History of Criticism* (Boston, 1978).

Gainsford, Thomas, *The True and Wonderfull History of Perkin Warbeck* (1618).

————, *The True Exemplary, and Remarkable History of the Earle of Tirone* (1619).

————, *The Vision and Discourse of Henry the Seventh* (1610).

————, *Vox Spiritus* (1621), ms. fac. published by *The Rota* (Exeter, 1983).

Gairdner, James, *The Story of Perkin Warbeck* in *History of the Life and Reign of Richard the Third* (Cambridge, 1898; new ed.).

Gardiner, Samuel R., *History of England*, III and IV (London, new impression, 1901).

Goldberg, Jonathan, *James I and the Politics of Literature* (Baltimore, 1983).

Goodman, Godfrey, *The Court of King James the First*, ed. John S. Brewer, 2 vols (1839).

Gordon, D. J., "Rubens and the Whitehall Ceiling," in *The Renaissance Imagination*, ed. Stephen Orgel (Berkeley, 1980), pp. 24-50.

Hall, Edward, *The Union of the Two Noble and Illustre Famelies of Lancastre & Yorke* (1548).

Harbage, Alfred, "The Mystery of *Perkin Warbeck*," *Studies in the English Renaissance Drama*, ed. Josephine W. Bennett, Oscar Cargill, and Vernon Hall, Jr. (New York, 1959), pp. 125-141.

Harrison, Stephen, *The Arch[e]s of Triumph* (1604).

Harry, George Owen, *The Genealogy of the High and Mighty Monarch, James* (1604).

Heinemann, Margot, *Puritanism and Theatre: Thomas Middleton and Opposition Drama under the Early Stuarts* (Cambridge, 1980).

Held, Julius S., "The Union of the Crowns," in *The Oil Sketches of Peter Paul Rubens: A Critical Catalogue* (Princeton, 1980), I, 204-210.

Hogan, Floriana T., "*Elizabethan and Jacobean Dramas and Their Spanish Sources*," in David M. Bergeron, ed., *Research Opportunities in Renaissance Drama*, 19 (Lawrence, Kansas, 1977), 37-47.

Homan, Sidney R., Jr., "Dekker as Collaborator in Ford's *Perkin Warbeck*," *ELN*, 3 (1965), 104-106.

James VI and I, *Daemonologie* (Edinburgh, 1597).

————, *Letters of King James VI & I*, ed. G. P. V. Akrigg (Berkeley, 1984).

————, *The Political Works of James I*, ed. Charles Howard McIlwain (Cambridge, Mass., 1918).

————, *The Workes of the Most High and Mightie Prince, James* (1616).

Johnson, Richard, *A Crowne-Garland of Goulden Roses* (1612).

Jonson, Ben. *The Complete Masques*, ed. Stephen Orgel (New Haven, 1969).

Kistner, Arthur L. and M. K., "The Dramatic Functions of Love in the Tragedies of John Ford," *SP*, 70 (1973), 62-76.

Lee, Maurice, Jr., *Government by Pen: Scotland under James VI and I* (Urbana, Ill., 1980).

Leech, Clifford, *John Ford and the Drama of His Time* (1957).

Lindenberger, Herbert, *Historical Drama: The Relation of Literature and Reality* (Chicago, 1975).

Logan, Terence P., and Denzell S. Smith, ed., *The Later Jacobean and Caroline Dramatists: A Survey and Bibliography of Recent Studies in English Renaissance Drama* (Lincoln, Neb., 1978).

Luna, Juan de, *The Pursuit of the Historie of Lazarillo de Tormez* (1622).

———, *A Short and Compendious Art for to Learne to Reade, Write, Pronounce and Speake the Spanish Tongue* (1623).

Mathew, David, *Scotland under Charles I* (1955).

Mattingly, Garrett, *Renaissance Diplomacy* (Baltimore, 1964; c. 1955).

Middleton, Thomas, *A Game at Chesse* (1625).

———, *The Triumphs of Integrity* (1623).

Mish, Charles C., comp., *English Prose Fiction, 1600-1700: A Chronological Checklist* (Charlottesville, Virginia, 1967).

Munday, Anthony, *The Triumphes of Reunited Britania* (1605).

Neill, Michael, "'Anticke Pageantrie': The Mannerist Art of *Perkin Warbeck*," *RD*, 7 (1976), 117-150.

Nichols, John, *The Progresses, Processions, and Magnificent Festivities, of King James the First*, IV (1828).

———, *The Progresses and Public Processions of Queen Elizabeth*, III (1823).

Norbrook, David, *Poetry and Politics in the English Renaissance* (1984).

Oliver, H. J., *The Problem of John Ford* (Carlton, Australia, 1955).

Orbison, Tucker, *The Tragic Vision of John Ford*, Salzburg Studies in English Literature: Jacobean Drama Studies No. 21 (Salzburg, 1974).

Osborne, Francis, *Some Traditionall Memorialls on the Raigne of King James the First* (1658), in *Secret History of the Court of James the First*, I (Edinburgh, 1811).

Oudin, César, *A Grammar Spanish and English*, trans. James Wadsworth (1622).

Palme, Per, *Triumph of Peace: A Study of the Whitehall Banqueting House* (1957).

Parry, Graham, *The Golden Age Restor'd: The Culture of the Stuart Court* (New York, 1981).

Patterson, Annabel, *Censorship and Interpretation: The Conditions of Writing and Reading in Early Modern England* (Madison, Wis., 1984).

Paul, Henry N., *The Royal Play of Macbeth* (New York, 1950).

The Peace-Maker: Or, Great Brittaines Blessing (1618).

Perceval, Richard, *A Dictionary in Spanish and English* (1623).

Quarles, John, "Upon the Incomparable Tragedy Called *Mirza*," in Robert Baron, *Mirza* (1647).

Randall, Dale B. J., *The Golden Tapestry: A Critical Survey of Non-chivalric Spanish Fiction in English Translation (1543-1657)* (Durham, N.C., 1963).

————, *Jonson's Gypsies Unmasked: Background and Theme of "The Gypsies Metamorphos'd"* (Durham, N.C., 1975).

————, "Some New Perspectives on the Spanish Setting of *The Changeling* and Its Source," forthcoming in *Medieval & Renaissance Drama in England*.

Ribner, Irving, *The English History Play in the Age of Shakespeare* (London, 1965; 1st ed., Princeton, 1957).

Rich, Barnabe, *A New Description of Ireland* (1610).

Sergeaunt, M. Joan, *John Ford* (Oxford, 1935).

Slatyer, William, *The History of Great Britanie* (1621).

Speed, John, *The History of Great Britaine* (1611).

Stavig, Mark, *John Ford and the Traditional Moral Order* (Madison, Wis., 1968).

Stanley, Arthur Penrhyn, *Historical Memorials of Westminster Abbey* (1911; 1st ed., 1867).

Stradling, John, *Beati Pacifici: A Divine Poem Written to the Kings Most Excellent Majestie* (1623).

Taylor, John, *A Memorial of All the English Monarchs* (1622).

Tom Tell Troath (London[?], 162[-?]).

Tucker, Kenneth, *A Bibliography of Writings by and about John Ford and Cyril Tourneur* (Boston, 1977).

Ure, Peter, "A Pointer to the Date of Ford's 'Perkin Warbeck,'" *NQ*, n.s. 17 (1970), 215-217.

————, See also *Ford*.

Vega Carpio, Lope Félix de, *The Pilgrime of Casteele*, anon. trans. (1621).

Weathers, Winston, "*Perkin Warbeck*: A Seventeenth-Century Psychological Play," *SEL*, 4 (1964), 217-226.

Wheeler, Thomas, "The Purpose of Bacon's *History of Henry the Seventh*," *SP*, 54 (1957), 1-13.

Wikander, Matthew H., "StrangeTruths: English Historical Drama in the Seventeenth Century," *Genre*, 9 (1976), 193-214.

Willan, Leonard, "The Epistle Dedicatory," *Orgula* (1658).

Willson, D. H., *King James VI and I* (1956).

Wilson, Arthur, *The History of Great Britain* (1653).